T0153558

# INCULTURATION

Working Papers on Living Faith and Cultures

edited by

ARIJ A. ROEST CROLLIUS, S.J.

## X

This issue has been published in collaboration with the Centre for Coordination of Research of the International Federation of Catholic Universities (F.I.U.C) and with the help of the Konrad Adenauer Foundation.

CENTRE "CULTURES AND RELIGIONS" - PONTIFICAL GREGORIAN UNIVERSITY

M. Dumais, R. Goldie, A. Święcicki

# CULTURAL CHANGE AND LIBERATION
# IN A CHRISTIAN PERSPECTIVE

ROME 1992

1987 – First edition
1992 – First reprint

ISBN 88-7652-578-5

EDITRICE PONTIFICIA UNIVERSITÀ GREGORIANA
Piazza della Pilotta, 35 - 00187 Roma

*Marcel Dumais, o.m.i., born in Drummondville, Canada, in 1936, did his ecclesiastical studies in Rome (L.Ph.; L.S.S.) and Paris (D.Th.). Since 1968 he has been teaching Holy Scripture (New Testament) at Saint Paul University in Ottawa, Canada. He was Academic Vice-Rector of this University from 1974 till 1980. Since 1982, he is the Director of the Mission Studies Institute of Saint Paul University. In 1984 he was appointed by the Pope member of the Pontifical Biblical Commission. He published a few books and many articles in French on New Testament topics, particularly on Evangelization in the Acts of the Apostles. He has been lecturing in a few Universities and has held numerous biblical sessions and retreats in various countries.*

*Rosemary Goldie was born in Sydney, Australia, in 1916. She studied at Sydney University and the Sorbonne (Paris). Since 1946 she has been involved in international work: in the Catholic student movement, in the organization of the World Congresses for the Lay Apostolate, and as Associate Secretary of the "Consilium de Laicis" of the Holy See. Since 1977 she has been lecturing at the Pontifical Lateran University on topics related to the laity in the mission of the Church.*

*Andrzej Święcicki, born in Belorussia (1915), Dr. hab., ret. professor of Social Sciences, since 1985 Head of the Department of Sociology of Religion in the Theological Academy of Warsaw. He is the author of works concerning alcohology, Christian social thought and the sociology of religion. Since 1972 he is the President of the Club of Catholic Intellectuals in Warsaw, the largest independent organization of Catholic lay people in Poland.*

# TABLE OF CONTENTS

Presentation by ARIJ A. ROEST CROLLIUS, S.J. . . . . . . . .   IX

MARCEL DUMAIS, o.m.i., "The Church of the Apostles: a
    Model of Inculturation? . . . . . . . . . . . . . . .   1

ROSEMARY GOLDIE, "The Christian Experience of Women in
    the Midst of Cultural Change" . . . . . . . . . . .   25

ANDRZEJ SWIĘCICKI, "Moral Polarization of Cultures"  . . .   47

# PRESENTATION

## CULTURE CHANGE AND THE LIBERATION OF THE HUMAN PERSON

Not all cultural change brings about a better human society. Not every human society that finds itself in a process of cultural change offers to its members greater freedom. Cultural change can also be a process of degeneration. Human persons who are involved in such a process risk becoming the slaves of their own conquests.

The endeavour of inculturation does not directly address itself to the individual human person, but rather to persons insofar as they form together a structured human society. Such a society has its values and traditions, its customs and expectations, its norms and stereotyped ways of interaction. However, all these elements and aspects of the cultural reality of a given society do not exist without the human persons that form that society. Each human person contributes to the culture in which he [or she] exists, and hands it on to the next generation.

At the same time, it can be said that the human person is the point of convergence of the values, norms and customs of a culture. This, because the person is not only part of human society, but transcends society in virtue of the uniqueness of his [or her] spiritual trascendentality. Culture, therefore, created and handed on by human persons, has as its final scope the perfection of the person in its freedom to unhindered development of the own identity and free communication of itself to other persons.

Christian revelation and the experience of history concur in establishing the fact that, in this process of growth and development, human beings have to reckon with a profound wound in their own history and existence. Hence, the process of change is always in peril of becoming a process of degeneration. And yet, in the perspective of the Christian faith, each human being is called to share in the very life and existence of God. Thus, the entire human history can be conceived as an immense workshop for the divinisation of human persons and society.

Inculturation is one of the aspects of the work that is going on in this workshop. It is the becoming present of the Christian life and message in human cultures, the re-shaping of these cultures according to Christian values, and the establishing of a communion among all human societies and cultures in God's people on earth on its pilgrimage to the heavenly homeland.

This series of working papers opens with the study on cultural change in the process of evangelization according to the Acts of the Apostles. The two other articles deal with more personal aspects of this process: the role of women and the moral implications of inculturation. The papers were discussed at the "Jerusalem Seminar of the F.I.U.C. in 1985.

The paper of Professor Marcel Dumais, o.m.i., intends to define the relationship between faith and culture according to the Acts of the Apostles. The author makes clear that Jews who became Christians (Jesus' disciples, Paul and the converts after Pentecost) continued to live according to the customs and traditions they had received from Judaism. In regard to pagans who had become Christians the position taken by Acts is equally clear and firm: the laws and traditions characteristic of Judaism are not to be imposed on them. To become a Christian one does not have to turn oneself into a Jew first. The missionary discourses that offer us models of the evangelization process show that the relation of faith to culture is not simple. The missionary process in both the pagan Greek and Jewish milieux proceed from and worked within the socio-cultural realities that were charged with meaning for those addressed. However, the proclamation of the Good News also involved a criticism and a surpassing of the cultural and religious reality that they lived. One finds, then, three moments of the Christian mistery in the evangelization process: the insertion in cultures (incarnation), the critical rejection of their deficiencies (death) and the transformation of their elements (resurrection).

The article by Professor Rosemary Goldie deals with the hitherto almost unexplored role of women in the inculturation of Christianity. And yet little reflection is necessary to reveal the importance of "listening" to the experience of Christian women and involving them in processes of discernment. The paper illustrates the

X

irreversible trend towards greater self-awareness among women, even in the most traditional societies, and the relevance of this trend for inculturation. The "language question" is raised, and the questioning of Christian symbols by feminist theology. A chapter is devoted to cultural change in relation to religious life, especially in developing societies. Suggestions are made for further study and research.

The paper of Professor Andrzej Święcicki situates the process of cultural change in the field of tension between the divine, ultimate perfection and the process of human history. Cultural growth is conceived as an attempt to transcend the limitations of the "here-and-now" in the development of human capabilities. The Author sets out to show that there exist two one-sided approaches which he defines as "masculine" and "feminine". The unilateral, "masculine" approach strives for the domination of the material world, the exploitation of natural resources and the subjugation of other peoples. The one-sided, "feminine" approach tends to deal with persons and things in a more instrumental way, in view of their utility for the acquisition of material goods. The Author then goes on to show that these unilateral approaches can lead to pathological developments in individuals, families, societies and cultures.

With this issues of INCULTURATION we have almost completed the publication of the "Jerusalem Papers". A special word of thanks is addressed to Ms. Marina Paglino, the Secretary of the 1985 Seminar. With unabating enthusiasm and attentive care she collected the papers and prepared them for publication. We express also our gratitude to the Konrad Adenauer Foundation for making this publication possible.

ARIJ A. ROEST CROLLIUS, S.J.

Marcel Dumais, o.m.i.

# THE CHURCH OF THE ACTS OF THE APOSTLES: A MODEL OF INCULTURATION?

The problem of inculturation which was first posed in mission theology has begun to be of concern to biblical studies. Many exegetes, in fact, are asking whether the Bible itself is not where we should be looking for the foundation of inculturation and the criteria governing the insertion of the Gospel and faith into contemporary cultures. Consequently a certain number of biblical studies on this question have appeared in the last few years.[1] In 1979 the members of the Pontifical Biblical Commission dedicated their plenary working session to the study of this theme.[2] It was, moreover, in a discourse to the members of this Commission that a pope (John-Paul II) used the word "inculturation" in an official text for the first time.[3]

In order to make the terminology we shall be using clear right from the start, it might be good to begin with John-Paul II's observation in his allocution to the Biblical Commission that "though 'inculturation' is a neologism it expresses one of the elements of the great mystery of the Incarnation very well indeed."[4]

---

[1] Among recent publications: P. BEAUCHAMP and others, *Bible and Inculturation*, Rome, Pontifical Gregorian University, 1983, 125 pp. ( = Volume III of the series "Working Papers on Living Faith and Cultures", edited by A. Roest Crollius); C. STUHLMUELLER, in *The Biblical Foundations for Mission*, Maryknoll, N.Y., Orbis Books, 1983, chap. 2 "The Biblical Process of Acculturation" (on the Old Tstament). An ecumenical research group has studied this question: J. SCOTT and R. T. COOTE, editors, *Gospel & Culture*, Pasadena, Ca., William Carey Library, 1979, 469 pp.; the work contains some biblical studies but offers mainly anthropological and theological reflections.

[2] The contributions of the members of the Commission were subsequently published: PONTIFICIA COMMISSIONE BIBLICA, *Fede e Cultura alla Luce della Bibbia*, Leumann (Torino), Editrice Elle Di Ci, 1981, 343 pp.

[3] See *Fede e Cultura...*, p. 5. The Episcopal Synod of 1977 had already used the word in its "Message to the People of God", n. 5. Shortly after the meeting of the Biblical Commission John-Paul II used the word again in the Apostolic Exhortation "Catechesi tradendae" of October 16, 1979.

[4] *Fede e Cultura...*, p. 5.

Father Arrupe used the word in the same sense in his *Letter on Incisturation* (May 14, 1978): "Inculturation is the incarnation of the Christian life and message in a specific cultural setting." [5] This nominal definition seems to have received the vote of the majority today [6] and we, therefore, adopt it as our own.

What then of the meeting of faith and cultures in the earliest Christian period? The *Acts of the Apostles* is a privileged witness to this encounter. It shows that the problem of the inculturation of the Gospel and the Christian Faith was sharply felt in the primitive Church which very soon had to move from the Jewish world in which it had been brought to birth to a world that was pagan and, to a very large extent, Hellenistic in culture. Thus the question: should the way that the firat Christians responded to their problem not serve as an inspiration and a model in our own search for ways to live and to speak the Gospel in the context of our diverse socio-cultural realities?

In the following study, which focuses on Acts, we shall first consider the facts to see how the Christian faith encountered each ethnic group through its cultural and religious values. We shall then be able to make a more precise study of the relationship between faith and culture by observing how the first Christians proclaimed the Gospel to the Jews first of all and then to the pagan Greeks. We shall conclude by drawing out some guiding principles for a socio-cultural incarnation of the Gospel inspired by the praxis of the Primitive Church. [7]

---

[5] As cited by B. CHENU, "L'Evangile dans l'archipel des cultures", *Lumière et Vie*, 168, sept. 1984, p. 75.

[6] Always with variations. Some speak of the incarnation of the *gospel message*, others of the incarnation of the *faith*, and still others of the incarnation of the *Church*. The definition given by A. ROEST CROLLIUS demonstrates the position of the last group: "'Inculturation' is here meant as an expression of the process by which the Church becomes inserted in a given culture" (*What is so new about Inculturation?*, Rome, Pontifical Gregorian University, 1984, p. 2 note 3; p. 6); also see D. S. AMALORPAVADASS, in NBCLC Campus, *Milieu of God Experience. An artistic Synthesis of Spirituality*, Bangalore, 1982, p. 6.

[7] None of the biblical studies cited above systematically examine the text of the Acts of the Apostles with this question in mind. I have already published an article in connection with this theme in an issue of a review focused on the Acts of the Apostles: "La rencontre de la foi et des cultures", *Lumière et Vie*, 153/154, 1981, pp. 72-86. In taking up this study for the second time I make some modifications and additions.

## I: The Christian Life and Judaism

The disciples of Jesus and the first converts after Pentecost were all Jews. Consequently the Church first faced the problem of the relationship between Christians and culture in connection with the insertion of the first Christians into Judaism. The consciences of the first Christians faced two questions: Should they continue to live their Judaism fully now that they were Christians? Should Judaism be imposed on converts to Jesus Christ who come from paganism?

### A. *Jewish Christians and their Socio-Cultural Traditions*

The socio-cultural traditions of Judaism in Acts crystalize around four realities that have religious significance: the temple, the synagogue, circumcision, and the law.[8] How does Luke relate Jewish Christians to these realities?

First, some general observations. In Acts Luke never criticizes the Jews and Jewish Christians who have themselves circumcised and practice the law. Moreover, he cites no examples of Jewish Christians who have ceased to obeserve the law and to conform to Jewish traditions. On the contrary, he makes it seem perfectly normal that the first Christians, coming as they did from Judaism, should continue to live according to their cultural and religious traditions.

Look at the facts he reports. After the Resurrection and Pentecost the first Christians in Jerusalem do not stop going to the temple to pray (2,46; 3,1; 5,42). On their journeys in the diaspora Paul and Barnabas attend synagogues (13,14; 14,1; 17,2). Peter is anxious to live according to the customs he has received from Judaism (10,14). Stephen, who is accused by bribed individuals of disparaging the law (6,11 and 13), turns the tables on his accusers by reproaching the Jews for not observing the law "received ... through the ministry of angels" (7,53) and containing the "oracles of life" (7,38). Ananias, the disciple given the mission of seeking Paul out after his conversion, is described as "a devout observer of the law" (22,12). When Paul returns to meet the Christian Church

---

[8] Some studies of inculturation seem to forget that in the world of the biblical period it was true as it still is today in many African and Asian societies that culture and religion were so intertwined that cultural reality was a religious reality.

in Jerusalem after his missionary journeys, the leaders of this church are proud to tell him "You see, brother, how many thousands of Jews have come to believe, all of them staunch defenders of the law" (21,20).

Paul himself, the Apostle to the Gentiles, appears in Luke's work as one careful to remain personally faithful to the regulations of Judaism and even, occasionally, as one watchful to see that other converts from judaism do likewise. He circumcizes Timothy, born of a Greek father but son of a Jewish mother and, therefore, considered Jewish by Jewish law (16,3). As a result of a vow he made, no doubt the nazirite vow mentioned in Nm. 6,9-18, Paul had his head shaved at Cenchreae (18,18). In Caesarea some Jews who had come from Jerusalem accuse him of wrongs "none of which", however, "they were able to prove" (25,7). Paul defends himself forcefully, "I have committed no crime either against the law of the Jews or against the temple or against the emperor" (25,8; see 28,17 and 23,1-5). By going to the temple and beginning the rite of purification (21,26) Paul indicates that, contrary to the accusation brought against him, his teaching does not seek to push Jews in the diaspora to abandon circumcision and their other practices (21,21).

### Some Exceptions?

It may seem at first that two cases in Acts disparage the Jewish Christians' principle of conforming to their Jewish traditions. Peter is criticized by some members of the Christian community for entering the home of Cornelius and for eating with these uncircumcized individuals (11,3; see 10,48). Peter himself had affirmed "You must know that it is not proper (*athemitos*) for a Jew to associate with a Gentile or to have dealings with him" (10,28). What does the word *athemitos* that is translated as "not proper" signify? Its meaning is unclear. It may have the general sense of something outside the order of things or abominable, but not necessarily contrary to Jewish law (*anomos*).[9] Note that though there are laws in the Torah concerning unclean animals (for example, Lev. 11), there are none that describe pagans as unclean and that oblige Jews to keep socially apart from them. Is this verse

---

[9] S. G. WILSON, *Luke and the Law,* Cambridge, Cambridge University Press, 1983, pp. 69-70.

in Acts just a reflection of a widespread Jewish practice of the first century? In any case Peter justifies his new way of behaving towards the pagans by saying that God made him understand in a vision that no man ought to be considered unclean (10,28-29; 11,5-9; see 10,34-35). The pagans, therefore, are not included in the prohibitions of the Jewish law about what is unclean.

The equality that binds all humans together is at the heart of the revelation proclaimed by Jesus Christ (10,34-36). We know how important *koinônia* (2,42) was to the newborn Church to which Acts bears witness and that it found its expression, par excellence, in the eucharist communion ("the breaking of bread" of 2,42; 2,46; 20,7.11) which presupposes a table fellowship. It is clear that once pagans fully participated in the Church, Jewish Christians had to rub elbows with people who ate food that was unclean according to Jewish law. In sharing meals with Gentile Christians they even ran the risk of eating forbidden foods themselves. Compromises, therefore, had to be made. This seems to have involved a yielding on both sides. As we shall see, the converts from paganism were asked to abstain "from meat sacrificed to idols, from blood, from the meat of strangled animals" (15,29). These abstentions probably concerned especially, if not exclusively, the shared meal in the Christian assembly.

The second case which seems to be an exception to the ordinary practice of Jewish Christians concerns Stephen. His attitude toward the temple needs explaining. In his exposition he disparages the very existence of the temple and this may have been the main element in his discourse which led to his condemnation by the sanhedrin, the ancients, and the scribes. Stephen's attitude shows that the Judaism of the time was diversified and that this diversity was carried over into the bosom of Jewish Christianity. Stephen was part of the "Hellenist" (6,1) a group of Jewish disciples who were born outside of Palestine and who spoke Greek as their everyday language. The Hellenistic Jews had much less contact with the temple than the Palestinian Jews who attented it assiduously. Some of them had been affected by the criticism of temples and sacrifices circulating throughout the Hellenistic world of this period. It is also possible that Hellenistic Judaism had had contact with Essenism which was hostile to the temple of its period as the writings of Qumran show.[10] The negative opinion that Stephen may have had about the temple before his conversion was possibly strengthened once he learned of the criticism that Jesus himself had directed at the temple of his time.[11] Whatever the truth, his criticism of the temple does not necessarily imply that when he became a Christian he distanced himself from the way that he had looked at and lived his Jewishness before his conversion.[12]

A constant emerges from our survey of Acts: Jewish converts, whether from Palestine or the Hellenistic diaspora, felt no obligation, because of their Christian beliefs or the rites peculiar to Christianity, to stop living according to the customs and traditions they had received from Judaism (the sole exception being the sharing at table with pagan converts as the new faith required). This is why as long as the Jewish Christian group was dominant in the Church the Jews and Roman authorities saw Christianity as one stream among others (Pharisees, Sadducees, Essenes) in the midst of Judaism.

## B. *Gentile Christians and the Socio-Cultural Traditions of Judaism*

The Church took a decisive turn when some Hellenistic Christians who had arrived in Antioch in Syria abandoned the synagogue audience and preached the Gospel to the Greeks (11,20). Their effort was a success (11,21). This was followed by the success

---

[10] O. CULLMANN, *Der Johanneische Kreis. Sein Platz im Spätjudentum, in der Jüngerschaft Jesu und in Urchristentum*, Tübingen. J.C.B. Mohr, 1975; P. GEOLTRAIN, "Esséniens et Hellénistes", *Theologische Zeitschrift* 15, 1959, pp. 241-254 (see p. 253). One could also say that Stephen's Hellenistic point of view on the Temple is in harmony with an Old Testament current of thought found especially in the prophets for whom "the Most High does not dwell in buildings made by human hands" (Acts 7,48).

[11] M. H. SCHARLEMANN, *Stephen: A Singular Saint*, Rome, Pontifical Biblical Institute, 1968, p. 105.

[12] According to E. HAENCHEN, "Judentum und Christentum in der Apostelgeschichte", *Zeitschrift für die neutestamentliche Wissenschaft* 54, 1963, pp. 155-187, the criticism of the temple in Stephen's address reflects the situation of the Christians of Luke's time who had, at the end of the first century, completely distanced themselves from the temple and its religious value. This redactional dimension is probable but it does not exclude an underlying historical reality in Judaism and in Judaeo-Christianity before the destruction of the Temple.

of Paul and Barnabas who turned to the pagans after meeting difficulties among the Jews (13,46-47). The entry of pagans into the Church posed a problem that divided the Church for years: to become a Christian must one, first of all, become a Jew by undergoing circumcision and accepting the Jewish law with all its juridical and ritual regulations? The solution to this problem was made all the more difficult by Jesus' teaching on circumcision and the law which, at least as the evangelists have transmitted it, is unclear.

Nonetheless, the position of Acts on this question is unequivocal and constant: the practices and customs characteristic of Judaism are not to be imposed on pagans who become Christians. According to Acts, no non-Jewish convert, with the exception of the "God-fearers" who already adhered to certain practices of Judaism before entering the Church, submits to the traditions proper to Judaism, i.e. circumcision and the law, the cult in the temple or the synagogue. The Jewish Christians who wanted to impose the law and circumcision on them (15,5) saw their thesis rejected by the Jerusalem assembly (15,10.19.22.28). The conclusion of this assembly was of capital importance for the future of the Church. By deciding that a pagan who wanted to be a Christian did not have to become a Jew first, the Church opened its doors and became a place anyone could enter and live at ease in while maintaining his or her culture and customs.

Just as strongly as Paul remained personally faithful to his roots and Jewish practices, he insisted that these practices not be imposed on non-Jews. After the Jerusalem assembly Acts shows us no further challenges to Paul's position and no further efforts to impose the law on pagans.[13] When Paul appears before the leaders

---

[13] I cannot support J. Jervell's thesis that inasmuch as the Church is Israel restored, it is obliged to keep the law: "Luke knows of no Gentile mission that is free from the law" (*Luke and the People of God,* Minneapolis, Augsburg Publishing House, 1972, p. 144). According to Jervell, the pagans were integrated into the Church by their association with converted Jews who accomplish the promises and constitute the true Israel. He even writes: "The church *is* Israël" (in "The Mighty Minority" *Studia Theologica,* 34, 1980, pp. 28-29). Jervell's position, which initially stirred up much interest and even won the agreement of many biblicists, is now rejected by the majority of exegetes. It rests ultimatly on two passages of Acts (3,25-26 and 15,16-17), but it does not fit the texts of the book as a whole,

of the Jerusalem Church after his missionary journeys the accusation made against him is not that he counselled pagans who had become Christians to disregard the law of Moses or to leave their children uncircumcised but that he encouraged Jews living among the pagans to do these things (21,21).

### What About the Apostolic decree?

As regards the decree adopted by the Jerusalem assembly demanding, as James proposed, that pagans who have become Christians should abstain "from meat sacrificed to idols, from blood, from the meat of strangled animals, and from illicit sexual union" (15,29), it can in no way be interpreted in the context of the chapter as an imposition of the law. James sided with Peter (15,14-19) who had insisted that the yoke of the law, that all were incapable of bearing, not be imposed (15,10 and 5). The precise significance of each of the terms of the decree and the implication of the regulations in the literary context of Acts have already been the subject of numerous studies and the end of the writing on these topics is nowhere in sight. According to the most widely accepted opinion, the decree's regulations, which are concerned mainly with food, make sense in the context of Acts as an effort to regulate the practical question posed in Acts 11,3: what must be asked of the new converts so that Jewish Christians can share their meal without legal defilement. They lay out "that which is strictly necessary"

---

particularly those passages which describe the mission to the pagans and their entry into salvation as a fulfillment of God's plan manifested by the prophets and as an integral part of the Messiah's work (13,47; 26,23; 28,28; see *Lk* 24,47). The idea of presenting the Church in terms of (the true) Israel is foreign to Luke. The definitive People of God, i.e. the Church is not defined by race because it unites sons of Israel and pagans. On this discussion see especially A. GEORGE, "Israël", in *Etudes sur l'oeuvre de Luc*, Paris, Gabalda, 1978, pp. 87-125. J. DUPONT, "La conclusion des Actes et son rapport à l'ensemble de l'ouvrage de Luc", in J. KREMER, editor, *Les Actes des Apôtres. Traditions, rédaction, théologie*, Gembloux, Duculot, 1979, pp. 359-360 and 402-404. The positions we take obviously do not agree with many of the affirmations made by a recent author who heavily depends on Jervell's work: F. ROSSI DE GASPERIS, "Continuity and Newness in the Faith of the Mother Church of Jerusalem", in *Bible and Inculturation...*, pp. 19-69. We particularly have trouble with some of the affirmations on pp. 60-61 of this article. However we agree with the author's statements in his final pages (pp. 63-69).

(15,28) to make the common life possible. Those for whom the food prohibition are unimportant (Gentile Christians) ought to respect those for whom they are important (Jewish Christians).[14] The fact that the Christians of Antioch rejoiced when the apostolic letter was read (15,31) shows that the demands were not understood as an imposition of the law.

## C. *Each lived his faith according to his Culture and Traditions*

That is the conclusion that flows from our first approach to Acts. One could, with some adaptation, sum it up in the well-known phrase of St. Paul — let each one live his faith in the cultural situation in which he finds himself. In Acts, Luke relativizes the importance of the law. It is no more than a rule governing behaviour, the custom of a particular people, the Jews.

In this regard it is interesting that Luke is the only New Testament writer to use the word "custom" (*ethos* in Greek) to designate the law (Act 6,14; 15,1; 16,21; 21,21; 26,3; 28,17; see Lk 1,9; 2,42).[15] A similar use of the word *ethos* in the sense of *nomos,* the term usually employed to designate the law, is found in Flavius Josephus (e.g. Ant. XII, 281; XIV, 194-195). In his defence of the

---

[14] many interpreters see these regulations as an adaptation of the ritual prohibitions mentioned in Lev. 17-18 which the Israelites and also the Gentiles living among them must observe. Indeed, this is the *opinio communis* according to S. Wilson who studies the decree at some length in his *Luke and the Law* (pp. 72-102; see p. 76). Wilson offers some serious objections to this connection to Lev. 17-18 and, consequently, to a ritual interpretation of the decree (pp. 85-94). Two lines of interpretation seem to him more plausible and more in harmony with the immediate context of Acts (ch. 10-17): the rejection of whatever was connected with the pagan cults (the blood and meat of sacrifices, the sexual activities associated with the pagan cults); the proposal of ethical rules against the three major sins of pagans (idolatry, bloody actions, sexual immorality). If these two lines of interpretation are followed, the problem of the Jewish law does not arise. The difficulty in reaching a consensus on the meaning of the decree comes from the fact that in each of the interpretations one of the four terms poses a problem. In the food prohibition interpretation it is *porneia* (immorality) and, in the two interpreatations put forward by Wilson and other autours, it is *pniktos* (things strangled).

[15] In Lk 2,27, the noun *nomos* and the verb *ethizo* are united in the same statement which translates literally as "according to what is the custom of the Law".

Jewish people Josephus calls for tolerance of the laws of Judaism which he likens to the particular customs of any ethnic group (see Ant. XVI, 36f., 176f.). In the same way the author of Acts sees the law as part of the customs, i.e., of the culture of the Jewish people that must not, then, be imposed on non-Jews who have their own cultural traditions.[16] As a result the law is relativized even for Jewish Christians because its observance is no longer an essential condition of salvation (see 13,38; 15,11).

Respect for Jewish and non Jewish cultures and the non-imposition of circumcision and the law on converts from paganism no doubt indicate the situation of the Church at the end of the first century when Luke drafted his text. One can presume that the period of tensions and collisions between the two ways of envisaging the mission to the pagans lasted longer than the few conflicts described in Acts lead us to believe (chapt. 10,11 and 15). Whatever the case, Luke writes for his Church and calls it to live out a difficult pluralism as a Church composed of a majority made up of converts from paganism who hold firm to their cultural values and an active minority of Jews who have become Christians and remain faithful to the customs of Judaism.[17]


## II. MISSIONARY PROCLAMATION TO JEWS AND GREEKS

The relationship between this new reality, Christianity, and Judaism and the pagan cultures is not quite as simple as our study to this point may have led one to believe. An examination of the missionary discourses of Acts will allow us to be more precise about how Christianity encountered people in their socio-cultural and religious context.

It is widely agreed today that the missionary discourses of Acts were drafted by Luke who used traditional data reflecting the

---

[16] Moreover in Acts Luke uses the same word *ethos* to designate Roman customs (25,16; see 16,21).

[17] In his *Dialogue with Trypho* (n. 47) Justin is a witness to a similar situation in the Syrio-Palestinian church in the years 130-135. He asks Christians who have come from paganism to remain in communion with their Jewish Christian brothers unless these become propagandists for Jewish practices among the pagans and present these observances as necessary for salvation.

preaching of the first period of the Church to compose them. These discourses are presented as models of evangelization. Each of them forms a literary whole demonstrating a typical way to proclaim Jesus Christ either to the Jews as in the discourses of chapters 2 to 13 or to the pagan Greeks in the speeches at Lystra (14,15-17) and Athens (17,22-31).

Since these are supposed to be model discourses we might ask what essential message they proclaim. A comparative study of the discourses given in the Jewish milieu show that they all follow the same outline.[18] Each has a narrative, reflective, and interpellating stage. In general, each says that Jesus, who showed himself powerful in works and words during his life but who ended up on a cross, is now risen as witnesses can attest. Jesus is, therefore, the Christ, that is, the liberator of whom scripture speaks. Each individual, then, is invited to believe in him so as to enter life.

But by these discourses Luke not only wants to tell us what the essential *content* of missionary evangelization is. He also wants, and this perhaps more than anything, to offer us models of the *process* of evangelization to Jews on the one hand and to Greeks on the other. Each missionary discourse is, in fact, a language event in which a speaker seeks to communicate a Christian meaning to the auditors specified in the text. But, depending upon whether the auditors are Jews or pagans the process will be different because it will always be grounded in the socio-cultural realities that are charged with meaning for those addressed.

A. *Evangelization in the Jewish milieu*

Peter's discourses (2,14-39; 3,12-26; 4,8-12; 5,29-32; 10,34-43) or Paul's (13,16-41) directed not only to Jews by birth but also, occasionally, to "God-fearers" (10,34; 13,16) who shared the faith and piety of Israel, nourished themselves on the Old Testament and regularly attended the synagogue, are considered to be missionary discourses in the Jewish milieu. The great number of explicit references and allusions to texts of the Old Testament in these

---

[18] For a study of the content of what has been called the apostolic kerygma consult in particular the works of M. Dibelius, C. H. Dodd, J. Schmitt, U. Wilckens and J. Dupont.

discourses strikes one at first reading. These scriptural reminiscences which literally weave each Christian discourse together are drawn from the Septuagint used by Hellenistic Judaism. This leads us to think that these discourses were developed for Hellenistic synagogues in order to reach Jews in the diaspora. The method of argumentation used in these discourses relies especially on targums and midrashim and, though it disconcerts us, this mode of argument was familiar to the auditors in the synagogues.

Paul's speech in the synagogue at Antioch in Pisidia (13,16-41) may serve as an example of the typical process these discourses followed.[19] From the first reading of this text proclaiming Jesus Christ one is struck by the importance given to the Old Testament. The speaker begins with a résumé of Israel's history in which only the positive events experienced by the Jewish people are mentioned (vv. 17-23). This historical summary recalls the traditional creeds of the Jewish people especially Dt. 26,5-9. Right from the beginning of the discourse the Jewish listeners feel they are in familiar ground. The summary of the past concludes with a composite quotation of scripture that pays homage to David's spiritual qualities (v. 22). Further on the eye is stopped at verses 32-37 by another block of scriptural texts that speak of the resurrection in some way and seem to form the heart of the speaker's argumentation. Between these two sections there is a brief presentation of Jesus and his life with an emphasis on the resurrection (v. 23-31). The whole discourse hinges on verses 23 and 32. The same term and the same theme recur in these two verses in the mention of a "promise" made to the Fathers and now fulfilled by God in the risen Jesus.

This entire evangelical discourse is presented as an exposition and actualization of the Jewish scripture or, more precisely, of the text of the Davidic promise in 2 Sam. 7. The speaker talks the language of his auditors. he speaks the Jesus Christ event in terms of their culture, of their religious comprehension, of their expectations and their central hopes, i.e., in terms of the expectations and hopes associated with the promise of liberation and the coming of a new David.

---

[19] For a full development of what we are able to only evoke here, the reader is directed to the work we have written on this discourse: *Le langage de l'évangélisation. L'annonce missionnaire en milieu juif (Actes 13n16-41)*, Tournai-Montréal, Desclée-Bellarmin, 1976, 400 pp.

However, a more careful analysis of the discourse shows that, little by little, the speaker brings a new depth of meaning to the scriptural texts, to the cultural and religious values of his auditors and also to the hope they bear. The promise "to raise up" a new David (*anistèmi* in 2 Sam. 7,12) has become the reality of Jesus "raised up from the dead". (The same Greek verb, *anistèmi* is used in Acts 13,33 and 34). The whole process is based on a symbolic structure involving two levels of meaning given to the words and the realities they evoke. It is a matter of reaching a new and more profound sense by going from the commonly accepted meaning towards that to which they mysteriously allude. In the Antiochian discourse the speaker makes a new meaning emerge in a twofold way by projecting the light of other scriptural texts and the light of the lived event (the resurrection) on the promise of 2 Sam. 7.

In the familiar style of rabbinic exegesis the Christian speaker associates in verses 33-35 three biblical texts that share a verbal correspondence (Ps. 2,7; Is. 55,3; Ps. 16,10). None of these texts proves the resurrection of the Messiah. Each, however, points in the direction of the resurrection and sheds light on one of its aspects. When put together these citations interpret one another and clarify the text of the Davidic promise with a new light for the auditor familiar with midrashic argumentation.

But, if the texts of the Jewish scripture come to signify the resurrection it is, finally, only because the very event proclaimed (verses 30-31) uncovers the virtual sense they bear. In short, if scripture sheds light on the event, we are even more obliged to say that the event sheds light on scripture and leads to a new fullness of meaning. The auditors could integrate the Good news of Jesus Christ with the best of their culture and expectations. But they also had to make the decision to freely welcome Jesus and his resurrection. Christian living well involve continuity but also rupture and novelty.[20]

---

[20] Our brief probe of the missionary address at Antioch could also extend to the other discourses to the Jews which are likewise structures according to the literary form of "midrash", i.e. a reinterpretation of Scripture in the light of a new event. For example, the Pentecost address (2,14-39) is a midrash on the promise of Joel 3,1-5; Peter's argument for the resurrection of Jesus (2,25-35) is very close to that of Paul (13,32-37). The address in Acts 3,12-26 is a midrashic interpretation of Dt. 18,15-19; as in Acts 13, everything is centered on the double meaning the verb *anistèmi* can have, i.e. raise up (v. 22 quoting Dt.) – raise up from the dead (v. 26).

## B. *Evangelization in the Greek and Pagan Milieu*

With the brief address at Lystra (14,15-17) and especially the speech in Athens (17,22-31) there is a complete change of the decor, the audience, and, particularly, the form and content of thought. The scene is no longer the temple or the synagogue but the public forum. The audience is made up entirely of pagans who have grown up in the Hellenistic civilization. The speaker in Athens no longer draws his quotations from the Old Testament but from the Greek poets and philosophers. The discourse is not centered on the expectation of a Messiah but on the awareness of the presence of God in nature and in the midst of everyday life. The argumentation does not try to show that Jesus is the Messiah but that he is the instrument of God's judgment and the way that makes it easier for us to gain the difficult knowledge of the true God for which the very depth of our being yearns.[21]

We move now to a rather quick survey of the brief address at Lystra which functions as a literary preparation for the discourse in Athens. The Kerygma is incomplete since Jesus Christ is not proclaimed. Paul says to these people, who take himself and Barnabas for gods descended from heaven (vv. 11-12), that the God he reveals to them is already present because he made them (v. 15b) and he has always mysteriously directed their people and its history (v. 16) and, finally, it is he who regularly sends the rains and gives the land its fertility so that it might feed the people (v. 17). However, to recognize this true God they must abandon the false gods they have a tendency to fabricate (vv. 11-12 and 15a).

The speaker begins, then, with the actual religion of the people. He proclaims no other God than the one who is already present in their leves. The people of Lystra were able, therefore, to recognize

---

[21] The Athenian discourse is structured in two sections, the second (17,30-31) corresponding to the first (17,23-30). In fact, verses 23 and 30 correspond on the verbal level "To a God *Unknown...* what you are thus worshipping in *ignorance* I intend to *make known* to you (v. 23); "God may well have overlooked bygone periods when men *did not know* him, but he *calls* now" (v. 30). See P. AUFFRET, "Essai sur la structure littéraire du discours d'Athènes (Ac XVII 23-31)", *Novum Testament* 20, 1978, pp. 185-202; J. DUPONT, "Le discours à l'Aréopage (Ac 17,22-31) lieu de rencontre entre christianisme et hellénisme", *Biblica* 60, 1979, p. 541.

themselves in the God of Jesus Christ. The missionary discourse is well rooted in a precise social group which is agricultural, animist in inclination and which already recognizes a creator who is master of the rain just as he is in control of the destiny of the group.

Exegetes have long been divided on the interpretation to be given to Paul's discourse on the Areopagus of Athens. For some the discourse is typically Greek, for others the Old Testament and Judaism provide the background of the discourse's thought and argumentation.[22] Do we really have to choose between these two interpretations? The missionary discourse is, in its intentionality and literary form, essentially the reality of a speaker communicating a meaning to his auditors. The Athenian discourse is a good example of "transcultural" evangelization. A Christian speaker imbued with Jewish religious culture endeavours to communicate the faith to auditors belonging to the pagan Greek culture. What has meaning for the speaker within his cultural horizon must now take on meaning within their own socio-cultural horizon.

If one listens to the Athenian discourse with "Greek ears" the whole text makes sense without any need to step outside one's cultural and religious universe. Moreover, it is easier to make connections with Greek thought than with Jewish thought. From the start of his discourse the orator speaks of the "cosmos" (v. 24), a term that is found nowhere in the Old Testament. The presentation of God as creator of the world (v. 24) was current in the great Greek philosophers. The affirmation that God "does not dwell in sanctuaries" (v. 24) nor "receive man's service as if he were in need of it" (v. 25) calls to mind passages in Euripides and especially some themes dear to Stoic philosophers such as Zeno, Seneca, and Epictetus. The Stoics also proclaimed that God "gives to all life and breath" (v. 25), that he is not someone distant (v. 27) and that it is every man's vocation to seek him (v. 26). The heart of the discourse's argumentation is formed by verse 28 which refers to two Greek poets: "In him we live and move and have our being" echoes the poet Epimenides of Knossos and "for we too are his offspring" is a quotation of the Stoic poet Aratus. Even the Greek

---

[22] Some authors who have brought out the parallels with Hellenistic literature: E. Norden, M. Dibelius, M. Pohlenz, H. Hommel and E. des Places. B. Gärtner and A.-M. Dubarle highlight instead the parallels with Jewish literature.

verb *metanoein* at the end of the discourse (v. 30) seems to have more the Greek resonance of "to change one's way of seeing" than the biblical "to repent". In short, almost all the elements of the discourse evoke themes that were present in Stoicism, the popular philosophy of that era whose terminology and thought had impregnated all levels of society somewhat as Marxism has in many countries today.[23] Consequently the whole development of the missionary discourse could be understood by a Greek without any knowledge of the Old Testament.

However, the development of the discourse also fits within the Jewish Christian missionary's horizon of meaning. One could take each of the verses and find parallels in the vast literature of the Old Testament. The discourse will then appears as an expositition of biblical monotheism to the pagans, as a presentation of the one, provident God of the Old Testament, and as a criticism of idolatry according to a familiar pattern of thought found in the Old Testament and Judaism. One can say that the affirmation that God is close to man because he is his offsprings (vv. 27-28) recalls the biblical theme of man as the image of God just as much as the Stoic notion of the soul's relationship to God. The Greek wording of verse 26 is also ambiguous and translations, which have to make a choice, never manage to convey its complex meaning: the reference can just as well be to the historical providence of God over the lives of people (the Old Testament line) as to the order of nature as a manifestation of God (the Stoic line).[24] Humanity's vocation to seek God (*dzètein ton theon*) mentioned in verse 27 can be understood as a quest of the mind (its meaning in Hellenism) or as a quest of the heart and will (its meaning in the Old Testament).

Such is the nature, then, of "transcultural" evangelization.[25] For the Jewish Christian speaker (the transmitter) the meaning he

---

[23] In the New Testament period Stoicism was much more than a philosophical system. It had taken on many features of an organized religion according to C. PREAUX, *Le Monde hellénistique*, vol. 2, Paris, Presses Universitaires de France, 1978, pp. 644-646.

[24] The very beginning of verse 26 says quite simply: "from one" (*ex enos*) without further specification. This can be understood as "from one sole principle" (Stoicism) or as "from one sole man" (Old Testament: Gen. 1).

[25] The adjective "transcultural" is between inverted commas because it is not being used in the sense defined by anthropologists such as J. POIRIER, *Ethnologie*

communicates has the Old Testament as the horizon of its precomprehension. For the pagan Greek "receiver" the meaning can only be based on and arise out of his Hellenistic cultural horizon. The two horizons of signification on which Christian meaning comes to be written belong to the dynamics of the evangelization dialogue. One can go further and say that the multiplicity of meaning in the evangelization discourse, that is to say the ambivalence and even the ambiguity of its language make the communication of Christian meaning possible because, by being evocative, the language allows a new meaning to arise which provides the auditor with access to the Christian world of meaning.

The evangelizing discourse uses persuasive rhetoric. The Christian option does not impose itself. There is a continuity between culture and the Gospel and also rupture and novelty just as in the Jewish milieu, but the rupture and novelty are even more prominent. The Good News brings with it a criticism of certain religious traditions of the pagan world. It makes its auditors see a contradiction between their profound desire for a God who is both creator and close to humanity, and the way they in fact fabricate external gods. It makes them realize they should abandon their useless idols (14,15; 17,29) and attach themselves to the one, true God.[26]

The difference between the two corresponding verses that mark the beginning and the end of the speaker's elaboration in the Athenian discourse (vv. 23 and 30) is characteristic of the transformation (*metanoia*) that is sought. At the beginning the orator speaks of the Unknown God in these terms: "what (neuter) you are thus worshipping in ignorance [that] (neuter) I intend to make known to you" (v. 23). Does the use of the neuter not lead us

---

*régionale*, vol. 1, Paris, Gallimard, 1972, p. 24. In the missionary context in which we use it we give it the etymological meaning of a "passage" of the Gospel from a culture in which it is already inserted to another where it seeks to be inserted.

[26] At the level of source criticism there is no doubt that the two Christian discourses in Acts 14 and 17 owe a great deal to Hellenistic Judaism which had taken up Stoic themes and built a whole argument against idolatry for use as missionary propaganda among the pagans. The Athenian speaker shows that criticism of idolatry was part of Greek tradition itself (as it was part of the Old Testament tradition Jesus took up).

to understand that the God whom Paul proclaims and with whom they already have a religious relationship (they venerate him) remains for them somehow undefined, a non-person and associated, indeed, with the world of things (idols)? Throughout his argumentation (vv. 25-29) the speaker presents two ways of considering God according to their traditions. The neutral way as a non-person finds its ultimate expresion in the idols made by man (vv. 25 and 29; *to theion* in v. 29 is also neuter). The relational way recognizes God as person and as creator (*ho theos ho poièsas*, v. 24) of the entire universe but especially of people (v. 26) and, therefore, it recognizes the relationship of each one to him (vv. 27-28). The speaker shows that these two approaches are incompatible. If they choose the second, i.e., God as a person who is both creator and close to humanity — an approach which expresses the best of their culture (quotations from poets in v. 28) — they should reject the first, i.e., the non-person god of the idols: "*If* we are in fact God's offspring, we ought not to think..." (v. 29). At the conclusion of the argument what Paul intends to proclaim unambiguously is God as person (*ho theos,* v. 30). But, curiously, it is non longer Paul who proclaims but God. Is the decisive revelation or, rather, the invitation to make the decisive step (God proclaims the universal need of *metanoia*) reserved to God himself?

Another new element: at the very end of the Athenian discourse (v. 31) there is the unprepared for entry of Jesus on the scene. What role does this last verse play in the whole discourse? It is hard to say precisely. What place is Jesus given in this presentation that has been entirely theological until this moment? The terms used leave room for ambiguity.[27] In the context of verse 30 Jesus may be seen as the one who enables us to overcome our ignorance of God. The description of him as one risen from the dead and as the instrument of God's judgment does not seem to rest on any Hellenistic expectation.[28]

---

[27] Must the ambiguity be assessed positively as we have thought it good to do in the rest of the missionary discourse?

[28] In fact, the only function explicitly attributed to Jesus, who is not mentioned directly, is described in these words: "God (...) is going to judge the world through a man (*en andri*)" (v. 31). What kind of judgment (*krisis*) is this to be? In the context of v. 30 (and of the discourse as a whole) the judgment in question seems to be a matter of knowledge (the right knowledge of God) rather than a matter of conduct.

20

Many rejected the missionary message (v. 32). Some, however, "became believers" (v. 34). Among them are two individuals who are no doubt important people because Luke takes care to name them: Dionysius the Areopagite and a woman named Damaris. Ultimately the results were as good if not better than the results of the missionary proclamation to the Jews in the synagogues.[29]

One last but important observation. The Athenian discourse offers us an example of *inculturation* but one which is, finally, only at the initial stages of *enculturation* and *acculturation*. The discourse shows, in fact, that when a speaker whose faith had been inculturated in Judaism appeared before a new cultural group he knew how to appropriate the language and symbols of this group. In reference to cultural anthropology this might be called "enculturation".[30] But then comes "culture shock" or acculturation. In fact, it is normal that the new culture that the missionary integrates reacts to his own as his does to that which he receives. Is this interaction verifiable in the Athenian discourse? We think it is. In knowing how to express his message in a language that made sense to each of the two cultural groups, that is, by finding a mutual, ambivalent, symbolic language, does the speaker not show that he knew how to widen each of the cultural horizons, to go beyond their differences, to establish communication between

---

[29] Following C. K. Barrett, let us also note the Greek construction *men - de* in v. 32, which suggests an opposition between two groups. The first group is made up of mockers while the second is made up of people who say: "We are so impressed by your message that we should like to hear it again" ("Paul's Speech on the Areopagus", in M. E. GLASSWELL and E. W. FASHOLE-LUKE, *New Testament Christianity for Africa and the World*, London, SPCK, 1974, p. 71). Some Bibles, notably the two most widely spread French versions, la *Bible de Jérusalem* and *Traduction oecuménique de la Bible*, continue to speak of the failure of the preaching at Athens and lead one to believe that Paul then had to change his preaching style by rejecting the ways of Greek wisdom as he says in 1 Cor. 2. It is bad methodology to interpret Luke by Paul. Recall that in Acts Luke wants to show the progression of the Gospel from the Jewish to the Greek world (see 1,8) and that, in working out this program, he offers typical examples of missionary preaching.

[30] The birth of a missionary into another culture can be compared to the gradual entrance of a child into his own culture (enculturation). The terms *enculturation* and *acculturation* (interaction of cultures) retain in this text the meaning they have in anthropology. See J. POIRIER, *Ethnologie régionale...*, pp. 24-25; A. ROEST CROLLIUS, *What is so new...*, p. 6.

21

the cultures and, by that fact, knew how to make the communication of the message of faith possible?

But inculturation properly so called is ultimately achieved only by the "receiver" of the message once he has accepted it into his own culture which is different from that of the "transmitter." But the discourse in Acts shows us only the "transmitter's" process not that of the "receiver". In reading the Athenian discourse with its symbolic opening one may presume that the message proclaimed is called to take on meaning in *a different way* within the cultural context of the evangelized than it did within the cultural horizon of the evangelizer.[31]

CONCLUSIONS

We can extract some criteria for the inculturation of the Christian faith from the praxis of the early Church described in the Acts of the Apostles.

1. The Christian faith is always expressed in a culture but it is not indissolubly tied to any culture, not even to that of Judaism in which it came to birth. The Christian faith can, then, be incarnated in all cultures.

2. If it is true that faith penetrates culture, it is also true that culture penetrates faith. Consequently each culture sheds light on new aspects of the mystery of God and Christ in order that its total richness may gradually be unfurled. The Gospel will be thought and lived differently by Jewish Christians in Antioch in Pisidia, converted Greeks in Athens, Europeans, South Americans, Africans, and Asians.

---

[31] The evangelization of the pagans in Athens was the beginning of the fulfillment of the program of Pentecost because it went beyond the geographical expansion of the Gospel toward its ethnic and cultural expansion. Every human being, in effect, is called to "hear the Word, each in his own language" (Acts 2, vv. 6,7 and 11). The universality of the Church is achieved gradually to the degree that each individual and each ethnic group hears the Gospel in his language, i.e. incarnates it in his culture of which language is the expression. At Pentecost people received the Spirit so that they could *hear* the Gospel just as the apostles received the Spirit so they could *proclaim* it (2, vv. 4 and 11).

3. Depending on the milieu and its expectations, the approach to evangelization will be Christocentric or theocentric. In the latter case the presentation of Jesus Christ, which often comes at the end of a long process, can take various forms to unfold the old or new richness of the person and the event of Jesus Christ in the creative and liberating plan of God.

4. In order to tend toward a real inculturation, the evangelizing discourse should pay heed to all the elements of a culture in their organic coherence and not just to some of them. But it should be particularly attentive to anything in the socio-cultural and religious life of the people that is capable of taking on deeper meaning. It is not just any reality of culture and language that can "take aim" at Christian reality. The God who is proclaimed should be perceived as above and in opposition to all the idols men always tend to fabricate, and as simultaneously transcendent (creator) and immanent (close to each person). The Jesus Christ event should be understood and lived as the total and decisive accomplishment of the humanity's hope of life and liberation.

5. The process of evangelization has three stages which are not necessarily separated in time: to accept, to go beyond, to criticize. To accept cultures and religions means, first of all, a willingness to listen to them and then to make an effort to understand them and, finally, to give them a positive welcome. A certain going beyond or rather a transformation of cultural and religious values will come about because the God of Jesus and the Jesus Christ event will be unveiled in their midst. The opening to Christian reality will bring wbout a progressive purification of the language and the socio-religious life of those to whom the Gospel is addressed.[32] The missionary proclamation will take care, therefore, to identify the values of cultures and societies but also be conscious of their weaknesses and the narrow confines in which they tend to enclose themselves.

---

[32] This is ultimately the work of those who receive the Gospel or, more precisely, of the Spirit who operates in and throught them. As I was finishing this text I came across a recent article containing the following sentence supporting my reflections: "La culture qui accepte de se laisser ainsi travailler de l'intérieur par l'Evangile se met à évoluer par elle-même, à se convertir, et elle produit *une réponse de foi qui est en même temps totalement évangélique (dans l'idéal) et totalement parole de cette culture-là*" (R. JAOUEN, "Les conditions d'une inculturation fiable. Observations d'un missionnaire au Cameroun", *Lumière et Vie*, 168, 1984, p. 40).

One finds, then, in the evangelization process, the three moments of the Christian mystery: the *incarnation* in cultures, the confrontation with cultures and the *death* of some of their elements, and the *resurrection,* that is, the transformation of cultures. In Jesus the three moments are part of the same movement, so much so that the incarnation does not truly reach its fullness until the resurrection, after the necessary passage thorugh death. To remove one of these three elements is to truncate the Christian mystery. The same is true of the whole mission of evangelization.

MARCEL DUMAIS, o.m.i.

Rosemary Goldie

# THE CHRISTIAN EXPERIENCE OF WOMEN IN THE MIDST OF CULTURAL CHANGE

Our research on "inculturation" is motivated by the need to allow the Christian message, the life-giving Spirit of Christ, to penetrate not only particular cultures, but the very process of cultural change. It may be argued, however, at least as a broad generalization that women even more than men, are deeply affected by — or resistant to — cultural change. On the other hand, in many "traditional" cultures, the status of women presents aspects that *must* change if a Christian vision of humankind is to prevail; while in modernized societies moving towards the "computor age", the human values most deeply threatened are those which — though by no means exclusive to women — are generally identified as "feminine", so that women's contribution would seem to be specially needed for inculturating Christianity into our technological civilization.

The contribution of Christian women to the necessary process of discernment as to what to keep and what to change in traditional culture, and what to do for the humanization — and Christianization — of modern society, will not, however, be given fully, and it may be wholly lost, if there is not within the Churches a conscious effort to "listen to" the experience of women (including the less articulate among them) and to involve them in reflection and decision-making. Many "feminist" positions have already been refined, and others may be abandoned with time, but the trend towards women's greater self-awareness is irreversible, and is progressively reaching even the most traditional societies. It is a factor that evangelization and inculturation cannot afford to overlook.

*Cause and effect of cultural change*

In the cultural "mutation" that has taken place, and is taking place in the contemporary world, accelerated by the unprecedented rate of development in technology and communication, the changing situations of women — in all their cultural diversity — are an integral part, at once cause and effect.

Not one will question the "effects" for women of overall cultural change, brought about by urbanization, industrialization, generalized access to education, and now by the advent of the electronic age. They are effects that may be for better or for worse. It would be a massive over-simplification to see *only* "emancipation" or "promotion" in these new situations, as though the women of past, or present, traditional societies were — or are — uniformly "oppressed" and stifled in every initiative, and the brave new world offers them, automatically, freedom and fulfilment in harmonious collaboration with their fellow-*men*. By and large, however, one can endorse a diagnosis made during International Women's Year 1975:

> The will to promote and the efforts to liberate women are among the outstanding phenomena of our time: they are helping to create a crisis in human society as it has been constituted for centuries and in most of its patterns of thought and behaviour, as much in interpersonal relationships as in groups, associations, classes, institutions, peoples and nations.
>
> Moving away from a type of society that laid all its stress on masculine roles, and forgot, or discriminated against, and not infrequently oppressed women, there has been a gradual change towards a new type of society in which women are evolving from a state of dependence to one of autonomy, from constraint to freedom, from passivity to initiative, from resignation to a desire for action, and from subordination to responsible participation.[1]

What emerges from this text, and what is not generally stressed, is that the new situations open to women, their new self-awareness and sense of responsiblity and their active participation in the tasks of society, are also among the *causes* of cultural change — and, once again, for better or for worse. The Pastoral Constitution *Gaudium et Spes* noted the "tensions" arising out of new social relationships between the sexes".[2] In the past

---

[1] Franco BIFFI, *Woman in a Society of Global Dimension: 1975*, a sociological study prepared for the Study Commission on Woman in Society and the Church, in The *Church and the International Women's Year 1975*, edited by the Pontifical Council for the Laity, Vatican City 1976, p. 119.

[2] n. 8.

28

twenty years, these "tensions" in the family or in the wider social context have often exploded in recriminations or frustrations; but they have also been explored, positively, in a search for new forms of "partnership " and cooperation.

The UN Conference for the close of the Decade for Women reviewed in Nairobi, in July 1985, the efforts made on a world-wide scale — and down to grass-roots of the "developing" countries — to meet the goals that were set at the 1975 Conference in Mexico, a Conference that was hailed by Paul VI as marking "a genuinely new stage in the progress of nations in their constant search for more just and human conditions of life".[3] At the half-way point in the Decade, the Pontifical Council for the Laity noted not only concrete measures to overcome unjust discrimination, but also encouraging signs of new attitudes:

> ... over the past few years there has been a much keener awareness of women's problems. Schemes have been undertaken to enhance the status of women in the legislation of several countries ... to rectify their "image" and do away with their exploitation by the mass media, and to help the most underprivileged, etc. In the West, and even in the feminist movements ... some of the purely egalitarian demands (women should be able to do anything that a man can do), or even the "anti-male" demands, have been superseded in favour of the desire to see a society in which each person, man or woman, can play a full part in developing the quality of human life, respecting real differences that exist ... The new concepts can have important repercussions on the overall education of people, on collaboration between men and women ... on efforts to ensure the balanced development of peoples and the influence of spiritual values among individual persons and whole communities.[4]

In a survey undertaken in view of the Nairobi Conference, followed by an International Seminar at Dar-es-Salaam (25 February-1 March 1985), Pax Romana — International Catholic Movement for Intellectual and Cultural Affairs — endeavoured to determine "the role and potential of professional women in

---

[3] Message addressed to Mrs. Helvi Sipilä , Secretary General of the World Conference of the International Women's Year, 16 June 1975.

[4] Working Paper in preparation for the World Conference for the United Nations Decade for Women (Copenhagen, July 1980), p. 4. Mimeographed.

development and societal change". The real problem is here. It is not just a matter of opening ever new doors to women (tough this must be done in many contexts), but of trying to assess in terms of quality of life — both for women and for men — the contribution that women can and do make to "more just and more human conditions of life". This is no mereley statistical task. Much is intangible, elusive. But even the effort to experience the changes that are taking place, if not to evaluate them mathematically, is part of a new approach, a cultural mutation.

*Relevance for Inculturation?*

What does all this mean for evangelization? for inculturating Christianity?

The working-paper of 1980, quoted above, points to a relevance of its remarks for the life of the Church:

> Within the Church in many places, sound progress has been made in involving women in the "services" of the Church community, particularly catechesis, discussing and planning of pastoral councils, theology courses that have been made more widely available... to both lay and religious women...

Alongside the extensive literature about women as the "second sex" within the "patriarchal" Church, there is, indeed, a vast and growing documentation on this positive involvement. More and more statistics are available about women — religious and lay — who are occupying positions and rendering services formerly inaccessible to the "non-ordained", much less to women. But to see the relevance for inculturation of women's changing roles in society at large we need to look deeper. Vatican II said already: "Since in our days women are taking an increasingly active share in the whole life of society, it is very important that their participation in the various sectors of the Church's apostolate should likewise develop".[5] Twenty years later we should be able to ask: When women are present and active, what do they bring? — Attachment to traditional ways within closed cultural horizons? — Sensitivity to the "new" and rejection of the "old"? — Solid religious values and

---

[5] *Apostolicam actuositatem*, n. 9.

a faith that is proof against cultural upheaval? How does their new self-awareness affect their religious experience? How does their new faith experience affect their relationships, their environment, in family, profession, work-place?

These are questions that can be asked in the context of Western Catholicism. They must also be asked in relation to the women of "young" Christian communities, and of those especially that are experiencing transition from traditional culture to "modern" life.[6] Even superficial observation can show that, in "developed" as in "developing" countries, religious traditions have been largely dependent on women's fidelity and womanly service.

In the Conclusions of the Asian Colloquium on Ministries in the Church, we read:

> Because of the important role the Asian woman plays in the family, her participation is of very great importance in the Asian context. In certain cultural settings only women can reach out to other women and exercise a meaningful ministry among them ... It is woman who can most influence members of the family. She plays a singular role in the formation of values and attitudes and in the upbringing of the family. Hence her importance in the transmission of faith, in building Christian families, in family planning, in the preparation and enrichment of marriage. In short, our Asian reality demands the presence and activity of women in all spheres.[7]

From the survey of the "role and function" of women in the particular regions of Asia, it is clear, however, that their "presence and activity" will not be able to fulfil the Bishops expectations unless genuine "Christian values" are made to prevail in the cultural changes that are taking place. There are exceptions: "In the *Philippines,* most likely due to Christianity and culture, the women occupy an important position, not only in the family but in the wider society as partners of men ..."[8]

---

[6] Cf. the documentation of PRO MUNDI VITA, especially Bulletins 56, 59, 83 and the special "Dossiers" on women in Africa, India, etc., some of which are quoted in this paper.

[7] FABC, *Asian Colloquium on Ministries in the Church,* Hong Kong, February 27 March 5, 1977 edited by Pedro S. De Achutegui, S.J., Manila 1977, p. 44.

[8] *Ibid.,* p. 208-209.

But, on the whole, there is a long way to go: *In India,* "women's status is secondary to that of men. Women have to be reborn; they cannot be saved. Woman's contribution, however, is recognized in her role as mother of a son (women on the male side have power)..." In *Pakistan,* "Many changes are coming in, especially among the youth ... There is no equality before the law, however, nor in religion; but this is simply accepted by the culture". In *Bangladesh,* "Women have to be married to exercise leadership ... In Christian communities in urban centers, where women enjoy more freedom, they run the risk of being looked upon as westernized". In *Japan,* women have the same opportunities as men as far as education goes, but after the university and in practice, they are "second class" citizens. In the home, however, woman plays a very significant role. In the new religions too, women's role is extremely influential".[9]

If Christianity needs to be actively present in cultural change where women are concerned, it must, however, be present with discernment. What has to be discerned is not only conformity with Christian teaching. There must be openness to women's actual faith experience. There must, as we said at the outset, be "listening". Preconceived ideas of inculturation can lead to unfortunate mistakes. Two examples come from a talk on "Women in the Church" by Pearl Drego, leader of the Indian group of the International Grail Movement.[10] The first is almost caricatural: "I heard a sister in North India complain that the priest wanted mothers who had just given birth to be allowed to lie on the mud-floor because that was the practice of the local culture. It did not matter if she got an infection and died". The second is of real significance for our study: "Too many church authorities are ignorant of the psychic structures of social events concerning

---

[9] *Ibid.,* p. 207-208. The last remark points to a phenomenon which would merit careful analysis from a pastoral point of view. It is confirmed in the Dossier n. 41 of PMV, *Women in Japan:* "Women, especially the middle aged women who have never been employed and thus have more time on hand because of smaller nuclear families and smaller houses or apartments, have created their own social circles usually centering on the local community and in many cases also on the small group activities in the so-called new religions... An amazingly high proportion of these religions have been founded by women." (p. 5).

[10] In "Vichar Vinimay", n. 30, December 1980, Bangalore, (Mimeographed).

women. For example, I find the Adivasi festival of the virgins is being christianized under the banner of inculturation without a proper anthropological and psycho-social study of the meaning this festival has for the young girls nor of the concept of womanhood that is contained in the rituals. While the ceremony makes beautiful associations of womanhood to nature, to new life and to motherhood, there is also a subtle defining of the task and goal of woman. She is being taught that it is her body that is of value to society and that she will find her service and fulfilment in society's expectations on her body as procreative and life-giving. She is being confined to a material role with mother nature and is denied her personhood and individuality."

### "More religious" than men?

Some one may object: Why all this concern about "involving" women and listening" to them? Is not Christianity, or at least Catholicism, already too "feminine" and too likely to appeal mainly to women? In a quite recent past it was common, in the Western world, to consider women as being "naturally more religious" than men — a judgement clearly revealing the gap between religion and mainstream culture.

In 1963 no less a person than Karl Rahner raised the question: [11] How does it come about that, in our Christian Europe, religion and religious life are more readily associated with the world of women? This "feminization", this "feminizing contamination" of Christianity in Europe — a Christianity marked by a typically feminine religiosity and piety — made it more difficult for men than for women to be "fervent Christians". The pastoral response to the problem was seen as requiring an approach that would avoid "overdoing" the demands of religious practice, respecting man's greater inclination towards the "transcendent", developing his sense of responsibility and being open to his more critical attitude. The implied psychology of "masculinity"as opposed to "femininity" and the sociology of relations between the public and the private sectors, between work life and personal relationships, would today raise many eyebrows (both male and female) even within the Central European context for which Rahner was writing; they would be

---

[11] *L'homme dans l'Eglise,* in "L'anneau d'or", March-April 1963, p. 93-107.

even more questionable in some extra-European cultures. But the principle of a pastoral approach adapted to personal and cultural reality remains valid today when the problem may even seem to be reversed, or at the least, new questions are being asked.

In 1984, Rahner's article was recalled in an American review of spirituality.[12] The article stressed that "masculinity" includes "femininity" that piety can be *too* "masculine" in the old sense, that "incorporating feminine images of God into a man's prayer may have significant consequences in the ways he relates to women in daily life". Meanwhile, grave voices are being raised to warn the Church that the women who have always formed the mass of "the flock" may be lost — are gradually being lost for want of attention to their aspirations, their needs, their position in the changing world of family, work, society.[13] The alarm may sound alarmist, exaggerated, but it cannot simply be overlooked. Society is changing *because* of the new possibilities opening up for women, and their questioning of time-honoured models. It is changing in ways that call for women's greater involvement and their creative insights. Rahner saw the contemporary, technological world as a "specifically masculine world", in which the "man of to-morrow" would have to practise a "specifically masculine asceticism", overcoming the "childish desire" to try out all the technical resources available to him.[14] Twenty years later, the inculturation of Christianity in the ever more technological society can be seen rather to call for the combined efforts of Christian men and women, for a mutuality of gifts and qualities that would make possible a balanced, and fully human approach to the world of "1984 and after".

*An Ecumenical Concern*

The need — the felt need — for this new approach emerges clearly from recent developments within the World Council of

---

[12] Mitch FINLEY, *Real Men Do Have Spirituality,* in "Praying", n. 5, Supplement to "National Catholic Reporter" (1984), p. 23-25.

[13] Cf. Archbishop Godfried DANNEELS, Primate of Belgium, at the 1980 Synod of Bishops, reported by G. CAPRILE, in *Il Sinodo dei Vescovi 1980*, La Civiltà Cattolica, Roma 1982, p. 206-7.

[14] op. cit., p. 105.

Churches. The "women's question" within the Council is not just a debate about access or not to ordination, but much more a search for new life-styles and new ways of "being Chruch" in cooperation between women and men.

At the Fifth Assembly in Nairobi, in 1975, the prominence given to the "issue" of "Women in a Changing World" was felt as a breakthrough. At the 1983 Sixth Assembly in Vancouver, women were no longer an "issue". But, "the symbols, the style, the witnesses given by women brought not so much analytical sharpness as authentic life experiences and committed engagement of women in the struggles of our time." [15] The Pre-Assembly Women's Meeting not only encouraged the "creation of a 'global sisterhood'", but gave an opportunity for the free expression and sharing of women's gifts and insights, in participatory Bible studies and worship, in singing and corporate actions. [16] This was felt to be necessary as a preparation for full participation in the Assembly itself; but the goal remained an "inclusive community of women and men". "To build a global sisterhood does not deny God's calling to women and men to belong together. But it opens to us women a deeper acceptance of ourselves and our sisters. Sisterhood lets us discover each other as women, non-competing, compassionate, true human-beings, to whom we can relate in deep friendship and joint commitment. It means that we take each other seriously as women. Only sisterhood and brotherhood together make a wholistic expression of our Christian faith." [17] This "goal" reflected the approach and the findings of a worldwide study on "The Community of Women and Men in the Church" launched from Geneva after the Nairobi Assembly and culminating at an International Consultation held in Sheffield, England, in July 1981.

One of the questions touched on in the study was the sharing of women in theological reflection and in the shaping of theological language. A particular field was that of biblical interpretation: "Now that women are beginning to read with their own eyes, bringing their own expertise and experience, we find that women are

---

[15] "Women in a Changing World", n. 17, February 1984, WCC, Geneva, p. 35.

[16] *Ibid.*

[17] "Women in a Changing World", n. 16, December 1983, p. 6.

able to see things that men have not been able to see, feel or recognize in the texts ... When we begin to hear Scripture with this new witness, it both helps to envision the renewed community of women and men and offers a foretaste of that community".[18]

Commenting on the importance of a "female point of view" in theology at the Pre-Assembly Meeting in Vancouver, "the Well", the Catholic Observer-Consultant, Maria Teresa Porcile of Uraguay, affirmed that women have a necessarily different perspective from men because they have three things men do not — a womb, a shedding of blood to give life, and breasts. "The womb is a space of life. The blood has a language in time, a sense of waiting and of hope in human growth. And breasts are for nurturing." Because of their bodies, women can provide a new way of talking about the mystery of God and the ministry of the Church. Women can help to make the Church a space of life, with a more natural sense of time and rhythm; and can nurture the faith. Like Jesus Christ himself, "women shed blood to give life to the world". Maria Teresa's viewpoint was supported by Mercy Oduyoye, a Ghanaian Methodist, from a traditionally matriarchal family. "The men say, 'African women are not oppressed', and the men speak for us in these international forums. But we have a saying that the person who sleeps by the fire knows how hot the fire is".[19]

*The "Language" Question*

The question of theological language cannot be indifferent for inculturation. The problem of "inclusive language" has been to the fore in Western society since the attack on "sexism in the '70' s".[20] We are familiar with the "chairperson" and we like to refer to "humankind"; and the search for adequate terms is occupying, and dividing, expert liturgists. But the question is not only one of words. It involves images and symbols, even the deepest levels of religious symbolism. The questioning, and even rejection of basic Christian symbols by radical feminists is well known. The Methodist theologian, Robert Hamerton-Kelly, writing in "Concilium" points

---

[18] WCC Central Committee, Dresden 1981, Document no. 1.3, Plenary Report on the Sheffield Consultation.

[19] "Women in a Changing World", n. 16, p. 31.

[20] This was the title of a WCC Consultation held in Berlin in 1974.

to two facts that must be taken into account by theology today: Jesus expressed his deepest experience of God through the symbol of "Father", while there are women who find this symbol humiliating and dehumanizing.[21] The problem, he goes on to say, is a real one and must be faced. Hamerton-Kelly is right. But, for the purpose of inculturating Christianity in the modern world, it would be rash to adopt the radical feminist stance uncritically, even within Western society. There are different cultures; and there are differences of mentality within a cultural context. In a panel discussion at the Pre-Assembly Women's Meeting in Vancouver, Pauline Webb, English Methodist and member of the WCC Central Committee, remarked: "I think we have not really gone deep enough into this language thing about the father and mother images of God, and I think a lot of women find the father image of God a very comforting one. It's one that keeps us immature because for most women, most daughters remain Daddy's little girl for the rest of their lives. Whereas Mother is the parent who expects you to take responsibility and be a woman. Now, it's the other way round for men ..." [22] The reasoning is feminist, but rather different from the usual anti-patriarchal approach. And, on this subject of the "language thing", we might quote a voice from Nigeria: "In Yoruba language we have images to describe God as both male and female — the female imagery is used in the context of idol worshipping, when the idol is used as the intermediary to God".[23]

The "language question" is raised at the deepest level by Maria de Lourdes Pintasilgo in *Les nouveaux féminismes*.[24] After analysing the "new feminisms", the Author shows them in an inevitable confrontation with the "primordial symbolism" of Christianity. The

---

[21] Cf. *Dio-Padre nella Bibbia e nell'esperienza di Gesù*, in "Concilium" (Italian edition) 3/1981, p. 167.

[22] "Women in a Changing World", n. 16, December 1983, p. 10.

[23] "Women in a Changing World", n. 10, June 1981, p. 6.

[24] Maria de Lourdes PINTASILGO, *Les nouveaux féminismes: Question pour les chrétiens?* Editions du Cerf, Paris 1980. The volume contains the text of five lectures given at the "Institut Catholique" in Paris, February-March 1979. The Author, engineer by profession, is a member of "The Grail", an international movement of Christian women. She was Portuguese Minister of Social Affairs in 1974/75, Ambassador to UNESCO for several years and, in 1979, Prime Minister of Portugal.

new movements "bring with them social conditions and anthropological concepts which are not without effect on the most fundamental images of the world of faith".[25] This Christian symbolism, derived from Bible, tradition and biblical interpretation, has grown up in a "patriarchal context". Examples are given from the "espousal" between God and humankind, from the creation story and from the image of the Father. The "masculine culture" underlying the primary Christian symbols is further seen in a conflictual relationship with the feminine element in Christianity in traditional Mariology and in the almost obsessional identification of women with sexuality and the ethical problems arising in the sexual field. As regards Mariology, "if Mary remains, for Christian women, an inspiration, it is not because of ecclesial institutions, but in spite of them". Today there are attempts to "redefine Mary's role in salvation history by careful attention to whatever, in her person and her history, comes close to the words the movements are saying today".[26]

It is impossible in a few lines to do justice to the wealth and the depth of the Author's reflections? nor is this the place to develop the reasons why the present writer does not go all the way with her in the intrpretation of Christianity's "patriarchal context" — while hoping not to succumb to the "idolatry" that Maria de Lourdes Pintasilgo denounces in the shape of "certain interiorized values, among them, that of man's superiority, which is perhaps the idol most cherished by women in her inner forum".[27] What is most

---

[25] "La symbolique primordiale chrétienne semble être ébranlée par les nouveaux mouvements de femmes. Ceux-ci portent en eux des conditions sociales et des conceptions anthropologiques qui ne vont pas sans toucher aux représentations les plus fondamentales du monde de la foi". (p. 98).

[26] Cf. p. 109-110. It should be remembered that Paul VI did some "redefining not too unlike that of the feminist writers in *Marialis cultus*, n. 37.

[27] Cf. p. 155. The interiorisation of this particular "value" can be a very real obstacle to healthy inculturation in the context, for instance of Latin American "machismo": "Perhaps the greatest negative fact in assuring the peasant woman's role as one of inferiority is the fact that she herself accepts her role as she accepts her female sex ... Many times her martyred acquiescence to this role leads her to become superstitiously religious, seeking her comfort in the Mass and the words of the priest who tells her she must endure her lot, for it is her role as woman, as given to her by God. Therefore what the peasant women might feel and what she is told she should feel result in a clash within her own personality, leaving her frustrated

relevant for our purpose is to stress Pintasilgo's conviction that, as a Christian woman who, at every stage of her reflection, must make an act of faith, she is also caught up in the "stream" of the new feminisms, and finds it indispensable to confront the questions they are raising.[28]

*Women Religious and Inculturation*

The interaction between the Christian experience of women religious and varying degrees of cultural change calls for a special chapter in our rapid survey. Why stress women religious? Not only because of their many roles within the Church — as "power houses" of prayer, "signs" of spiritual realities, educators, pastoral workers and evangelizers — but because, as intelligent women, often more spiritually aware and articulate than others, they are specially affected, both as individuals and as communities, by cultural change. The "varying degrees" of such change become evident when we pass from the search for identity of the indigenous African congregations to the escalation of radical change in many traditional Sisterhoods of the United States, dating from the "Sister Formation" movement of the 1950's to the diversely feminist attitudes and struggles of individuals, groups and "Conferences" in the '80's.

During the International Women's Year 1975, in the far-from-extremist context of the Study Commission on Women in Church and Society set up by Paul VI, the imperative of change in continuity for women religious called to the "apostolic life" was

---

and defeated." (Richard M. FAGLEY, *Easing the Burden of Rural Women*, in *UNICEF Assignment Children*, n. 36, 1976, p. 21).

In a different context, not of frustration but of holy enthusiasm, it would be interesting to explore the position within contemporary *North* American culture of the Charismatic Renewal Movement. The leaders — both male and female — while disclaiming any acceptance of "inferiority" or "inequality", firmly indicate "subordination" and "submission" as the key concepts for defining women's role in society and in the Church. (Cf. Stephen B. CLARK, *Man and Woman in Christ*, Servant Books, Ann Arbor, Michigan 1980; *Masculine and Feminine: What is the Difference?* An interview with Elisabeth ELLIOT, in "The New Covenant", February 1982, p. 20-23).

[28] Sister Claire HERREMANN, *Women Religious in the Church*, in *The Church and the International Women's Year 1975*, p. 95-104.

spelled out on the basis of contributions from different cultural situations. Amidst cultural change and at a time when all members of the Church are called to renewal, what remains and what changes for these women in their particular vocation?

What remains? — The call to follow Christ, to the praise of God, to fraternal life, to be "witnesses to the love of God", attentive to the problems of humanity "in order to respond to the needs of the poor". What changes? — The demand for greater personal responsibility, for greater nearness to contemporary men and women, for life in smaller communities, for fraternal collaboration with the laity at professional level, for social involvement in a world that is becoming more and more secularized. All this may raise problems, involve risks; it has repercussions on the way of living essential values, of practising obedience, poverty, chastity.[28]

If there is not sufficient openness for the impact of cultural change on religious life, there will inevitably be "crisis" for individuals, for communities and for religious life as an institution within the Chruch. If, on the other hand, cultural change becomes an absolute criterion, religious life will lose its authenticity. But, where there is adaptation with discernment of women's *real* Christian experience and their potentialities, religious communities can be, and are grace-filled and important instruments for inculturated evangelization.

During its 1977 General Assembly SEDOS[29] devoted a panel discussion to "New Insertions for Evangelization in Developing Societies where the Role of women is changing". One of the pertinent questions raised was: "Has the study of the changing situation of women in developing society and of the missionary response to this new situation a place in the formation programme of our candidates for the religious and missionary life? And in our ongoing formation programmes?"

*African Sisters in the Developing Society*

African Sisters have long been aware of the challenge of inculturation, if they have not always dealt with it in scientific terms.

---

[29] Documentation and Research Centre for Religious and Missionary Institutes of men and women (Via dei Verbiti, 1, 00154 Rome). The quotation is from the Report of the Assembly, p. 320.

"Why Do African Women Become Sisters?" The question was asked by "Sharing" in August 1971.[30] A PMV Dossier, intent on documenting the contrasting reactions of African women to Christianity, later suggested "comparing the women who became nuns with those who resisted the missionaries' advances. Were the former young and bent on a self-improvement which traditional structures impeded? Were the latter elderly and with a vested interest in the status quo"?[31] The writer went on to quote one authority[32] who "without wanting to detract from the selflessness of those responding to a divine call ... suggests that convent life being 'humanly, materially and spiritually an improvement on village life' counted for something in the vocations of the first Malawian sisters". In her answer to the question raised in "Sharing", Sister Mary Francis Mooya, of the African Congregation of the Sisters of St. Francis, graduate of the University of Zambia, admitted that there might be some truth in the contention that African women entered religious life to be liberated from the "man-dominated" African home and enjoy more wealth than other African women in the villages. This could not, however, be the main reason for the numbers of women responding to the call to religious life. A deeper explanation would be the "value placed on the vow of chastity" — even though "religious life is completely alien to most, if not all, African cultures and value systems", and its most foreign aspect is celibacy. When the vow of chastity was understood as "being married in a spiritual way to the Risen Christ", and so being also "a mother to all God's children", involved in His work" and "putting up with hard things for His sake", it would not conflict with tribal education — stressing motherliness, endurance and community life — but would rather be felt as an expression of "cultural values". And Sister Mary Francis concluded with a plea for "adaptation and interpretation according to our own cultures" while "preserving essentials".[33]

---

[30] AMECEA Pastoral Institute (Gaba, Uganda – now Eldoret, Kenya).

[31] Africa Dossier 9, October 1979, p. 9.

[32] I. LINDEN, *Catholics, Peasants and Chewa resistance in Nyasaland*, London 1974.

[33] "Sharing", Vol. 3, No. 6, *Religious Life – Sisters in Africa*, p. 10-11.

The interpretation given by Sister Mary Francis may be considered by some Sisters today as being *too* traditionally "cultural". In October 1977 the question of women religious was approached again in "Sharing". Sister Edel Bahati, of the Sisters of Our Lady of Charity, Nairobi, wrote: "There has been a great deal of growth in the life of the African Sister during the past six years. This evolution may not be seen in practical radical change perhaps. Such a revolution is yet to come. The evolution is in the thinking and in the minds and hearts of the Sisters. ... We want to be real and alive, participating fully in our mission as women in the Church and society in the present day. The days when a Sister lived a sheltered life divorced from the needs of the people are gone. The African Sister emerges as a woman of vision. I have been privileged to participate intensively in the workings of the Sisterhoods of Kenya in the past six years ... The period has seen the coming together of the Eastern African Sisterhoods (Tanzania, Kenya, Uganda, Malawi and Zambia) with observers from Ethiopia, Sudan and South Africa ... In 1971 the vital question: 'Has the African Sister really met Christ'? was raised ... It stirred up the desire to search further into the meaning of the consecrated life, the authenticity of the vows, the importance of prayer and the meaning of consecration for mission". Looking to the future, Sister Edel expected to "see the religious life changing radically in depth, not in externals". There might be obstacles. "The pleas of the Sisters to be given a chance to live their lives and order them in a mature way have reached the ears of the Bishops who desire to help as much as possible. But there is still some reservation. There is still the protective, paternalistic mentality with regard to the African Sister. 'She is not to be scandalised or be open to scandal; she is to close her ears to what she hears in case she absorbs wrong doctrine or theology'. I think this is appalling".[34]

From *West Africa,* Sister Eugenia Paidoo, Ghanaian, of the Handmaids of the Holy Child, echoed the call for a "more indigenous" religious life and "closer contact with the people". "How do religious become signs and witnesses to the people if they are cut off from them?"[35]

---

[34] "Sharing", Vol. 9, No. 4, *Women in the African Church,* p. 5-7.
[35] *Ibid.,* p. 8.

The problem of inculturation for women religious is complicated in many, probably most situations by a generation gap. This emerges very strongly in the experience of women religious in *Zaire,* as reflected during a Colloquium held at Kimwenza, near Kinshasa, 15-21 August 1979. The Colloquium was prepared by USUMA — Union of Women Major Superiors in the Republic of Zaire. It was attended by 45 Sisters representing the membership of diocesan and international congregations working in Zaire, with observers from Cameroon, Ethiopia and East Africa.[36]

The generation gap can be interpreted as the co-existence of a "Congolese" mentality and a "Zairian" one. Religious life inherited from the colonial past "a doctrinal, uniform view that dictated in the minutest detail the life of those who consecrated themselves to the service of the Gospel... However, the Zairian religious, post-colonial style, has developed quite a different identity. She now emerges as a far more complex person: partly due to the many and deep social changes of the last two decades... In various ways a number of indigenous congregations are trying to develop a life-style of their own in accordance with local tradition and mentality... Particular emphasis is placed on traditional hospitality, sharing and solidarity. These indigenous congregations effectively contribute to the evangelization of Zairian culture. They have understood the need to define the identity and the specific purpose of their young Zairian communities in terms... which relate to concepts familiar to the Zairian mind, e.g. the adaptation of wearing the national dress, *pagne,* and placing a totally different but relevant emphasis on partaking in family affairs."

In this way the first generation gap can be left behind. But, in the rapidity of social and cultural change new "gaps" can emerge. During the preparation of the Colloquium, lay people in Kinshasa were approached to give their evaluation of the presence and work of Zairian Sisters in present-day society. "Strikingly, Zairian society showed very little concern for the practice of obedience among the Sisters. Young Zairians look upon the practice of obedience in antagonistic manner and rate it as foolishness, alienation and humiliation. An ever increasing number of adults incline towards a

---

[36] Cf. PMV, Africa Dossier 14, May 1980 *Religious Life for Women in Zaire,* based on the Report of the Colloquium by Mary Hall.

similar view. This phenomenon is the more striking as it contrasts starkly with traditional norms... The Zairian Sisters clearly discerned that the dangerous trend might carry over into religious life and warned people against it..." It is to be hoped that this type of discernment is developing to meet the impact of secularization. At the Colloquium Sisters showed themselves as being still all too timid in making use of personal observation, reflection and judgement. "It is the competence of *bishops and African theologians*", we read, "to search, study and define the elements of African culture which are in harmony with the Gospel and which are to be integrated into the religious life of Africa and Zaire". That is very true, but the defining must not be done without reference to the experience of African Sisters.

In *India,* according to an Indian religious, Mother M. Digna, Superior General of the Carmelite Sisters of St. Teresa, the generation gap is complicated by "a difference of educational levels".[37] Authority especially is in crisis.

> "The older Sisters cannot easily grasp the new message... but accustomed as they are to obedience and to looking at all in authority as God's representatives, they do not oppose the new trends. The middle aged are aggressive and oppose the change... The younger are in the stream of it and like to swimm along with the current. They have learnt something but have not integrated the knowledge acquired nor reflected on the truths. They have been brought into an altogether new world: from a conservative rural background to an urban setting where modernisation is at work; from traditional piety to a Church open to change, free and all embracing; from a philosophy of passive quietism based on the past to a dynamic on-going future. They have learnt but have not interiorised. They speak with authority and their emphasis is on personality development, self determination, subsidiarity and responsible obedience. Personality development becomes the goal of religious life; community and its interests are thrust aside. Superiors intuitively know that this is not the way, but they are... unable to give the right direction... They ask for an on-going formation for themselves and the Sisters... They emphasise the need for a deep faith formation. They ask, above all, that Indian religious leaders, true to the tradition of the country, be prophets and 'sages' — 'rishis' who embody in themselves their ideal, Jesus Christ."

[37] *Authority and Leadership in Transition in the Context of Indian Women Religious,* in "UISG Bulletin", Number 66, 1984, p. 50-55.

Father Michael Amaladoss, S.J., speaking in June 1984 at a meeting on "Inculturation" held in Rome between representatives of the Congregation for the Evangelization of Peoples and of the Superiors General of Congregations for men and for women, remarked that in India, "where the Gospel comes in various European cultural garbs and the culture is animated by many great religions, inculturation is an inter-cultural and inter-religious project". It is "the task, not of a few expersts, but of the people". And "the people are looking for a *Word* that will transform their present life". But, the Word "emptied Himself and even died before He rose again to new life". One of the obstacles to authentic inculturation is the fear and insecurity that clings to the past". Are religious Congregations ready for self-emptying? Some at least are. Where religious houses tended in the past to become "islands of affluence", today "weave more and more groups, especially of women religious, living with the people, working with them, building them up, helping them, witnessing to their faith in a quiet way". This calls for a formation that is "experience-based", for a serious effort to "inculturate spirituality" and for theological reflection.[38]

*Return to the Source*

At the outset of our research — a fragmentary, "impressionistic" research, with no scientific pretensions — we stressed the need to "listen" to the Christian experience of women. The "listening" is needed in the effort to discern what should be kept and what must change in traditional cultures if the way is to be opened wide for the Christian message. It will be increasingly necessary in the ongoing process of humanizing and penetrating with Christian values our technological "post-industrial" society.

If we "listen" well, we may hear encouraging voices that promise a new Christian authenticity. They come in the efforts of more and more women to make direct contact with the Word of God, to meet Jesus in the Gospels, and gradually to make their

---

[38] Michael AMALADOSS, S.J., *Inculturation,* in SEDOS Bulletin 84/No. 13, p. 304-307.

experience articulate for themselves and for the Christian community. They need to do this within the tradition of the Church and helped by the riches of biblical scholarship — to which some are becoming able to contribute; they need above all to be open for the action of the Spirit, who can speak also through them. They are discovering how Jesus dealt with the women who followed and served him, and how women of the early Christian communities were present in the first inculturation of Christianity. This message has been somewhat obscured over the centuries, in spite of the great women mystics and the two "Doctors", who dealt familiarly with their Lord. But today, in whatever garb or at whatever level of culture, Christian women are needed who can help to "bring Christ" because they have truly met him.

ROSEMARY GOLDIE

ANDRZEJ SWIĘCICKI

# MORAL POLARIZATION OF CULTURES

This paper attempts an interpretation of processes that cause pathological development in cultures and their moral polarization. These considerations then lead to a heuristic model of cultural processes illustrated by examples drawn from the social sciences.

Although the paper was written from the standpoint of sociology, reference to the Bible is pivotal for it. The Bible is thus seen as one of the oldest and the most comprehensive document of human culture. Apart from the fact that for Christians it is the source of their faith, it also outlines the knowledge of its authors about man and human society. Finally, the evils undermining different cultures are contrasted with the moral demands of the Gospel.

## 1. Man as the Author of Culture, and His Fall

1.1. According to the book of Genesis God put man in command of the earth, which was organized in conformity with the principles of reason and adapted to man's needs. Everything was done "very well' (Gen. 1:27-31). In the religious thinking of almost all peoples there is the awareness of the eternal, omnipresent and almighty God, of His perfection and His transcendence with regard to man.

On the other hand, the cosmos as well as man himself have:

(a) a *beginning in time* and existential "now";

(b) a *place* under "heaven", i.e. their own "here";

(c) their own *"earth"*. i.e. their proper particle of matter, their own body with limited potential and mobility.

Since the Fall the religious awareness of God's perfection has gradually waned. But even so, in man's consciousness there is always a tension between the unlimited being of God and the limitations of everything material due to the passing of time, to the form and place occupied in space and to the limitation of energy. The tension generates and feeds the formative processes of culture. From the standpoint adopted here it is possible to distinguish between three kinds of these processes as they have successively appeared in historical consciousness and now exist concurrently:

(1) striving for the perpetuality of whatever in the surrounding world man finds to be useful for himself;

(2) imparting the desirable shape to the material and overcoming the distances separating persons and things;

(3) mastering the laws of causality in order to control increasingly powerful resources.

It is in this way that culture is created by *homo rationalis*.

1.2. God created not one but two separate human beings: man and woman. They differ not only in sex, unlike animals. In the description of creation mention is made of species of plants and animals but there is never any reference whatever to their sex (Gen. 1-2). But the Bible repeatedly stresses the separate creation of man and of woman (Gen. 1:27; 5:2). It seems, therefore, that the authors of the book of Genesis wanted to note not so much the difference in sex as the difference in kind of the two persons created by God and the dialogue to be established between them, a dialogue intended to generate a communion between persons. Without flesh the human person can be complete neither in this nor in the other world. But bodies differ; they can be either male or female. Everybody has from God a soul of the same kind and of the same dignity, while the body is inherited from the parents. It is the law of nature that decides whether a conceived child will be man or woman.

Organisms are termed *male* when they produce seeds and *female* when they produce the substrate, the ovum, in which, as in soil, the seed can develop. The contacts of the human person with the world as well as with other persons are established by means of the body. This is why in his dealings with the visible reality man treats it in two ways — either masculine or feminine. It is seen either as matter that can be dominated, that is the object of action, or as things and phenomena of varying usefulness, and, when it is a product of another person's action, as something characteristic of the acting subject.

50

The characteristic traits of woman's cultural personality are thus to perceive and to try to understand what in the experience of the external world is seen as a trace, a product or a sign of the acting person — whether divine or human — as well as to judge and to choose among things and persons. The characteristic trait of the male personality is, on the other hand, to view the external world as subordinate, as the soil to be tilled by actions of man. Referring to this difference the authors of Genesis described how Adam, the man, having been created first was presented with the external world for inspection and description (Gen. 2:19-20). He perceived the woman as somebody else, but still somebody of his own kind, whose inner structure was derived from his — as is symbolized by the rib. Not so the woman; first she sees her husband and then she sees the serpent and understands what it is telling her (Gen. 3:1-5). This biblical description shows relations among intelligent beings; its purport is the emergence of *homo socialis* as the last stage of creation. Interpersonal relations, communication and mutual assistance occupied the time spent in the garden of Eden by the first ultimately formed human beings.

The difference of the roles played by men and women in the communal creation of culture shows a solely statistical regularity. The powers of the soul are of the same kind in all human beings. The soul gives form to the body and can thus control it and make use of it with regard to the external world in ways characteristic for both men and women. There is, however, a high probability that the man and the woman will each follow his or her own proper way in building culture. The natural expansion of culture rests on the concurrent growth of both these pillars.

1.3. Man's turning away from the divine commandment disrupted this natural, simple pattern for the growth of culture. In disaccord with the "original covenant" a break-down occurred in the awareness of God's perfection and His transcendence of created human beings, as well as in the domination of nature by man and woman alike (Gen. 1:27-30). In natural morality good consisted in man's relations with other persons — divine or human — while his relation to nature was seen from the point of view of its usefulness. This natural boundary was obliterated when man deemed that to judge nature in terms of good and evil would give him knowledge that would make him the equal of God (Gen. 3:4-6). According to the biblical authors the woman incurred the punishment of pain and affliction from her children and husband, i.e. hers was the domain of culture dealing with the attitudes towards the actions of others. Man, on the other hand, instead of enjoying the transformation of nature had henceforth to experience the toil and fruitlesness of his labours.

The discord between the two pillars in the growth of culture has weighed heavy upon the history of mankind. Individuals, communities or societies with prevalent feminine traits, which allowed them to judge and to anticipate the behaviour of other people, thus had the ability to guide the "others", to hire them and treat them as instruments serving the acquisition of material wealth and helping to foster hedonism. Individuals and societies with prevalent masculine traits applied the available material means not only to command the earth but also to dominate other people; thus applied the material means brought homicide, violence and slavery. These differences and discords occur in all human communities and societies, beginning with marriage and family and reaching right up to the largest contemporary cultural formations. The author of the Apocalypse attributes the masculine traits to the formation he calls "the beast" and the feminine ones to what he calls "the great harlot" (Apoc. 13 and 17). Christian thought thus tends to see the history of mankind as a whole in terms of the division discussed here.

## 2. The different kinds and varieties of Culture

Among the connotation of the word "culture" there is man's search for definite values. Of these the ones here defined as fundamental are to overcome the limitations of time, space and to limitation of energy, and to integrate in society people who differ by their masculine or feminine attitude to the world.

The earliest cultures were those of groups, which sought as a fundamental value to surpass their own existential "now". Starting with the tradition of their past and in pace with the progressing rhythm of changing generations they strove for the future; such were the clans guarding the allegiance to their totem and kin-groups venerating the extraordinary deeds of their ancestors. In the next epoch of history the aspiration to expand one's own existential "here" became more prominent and more common. The knowledge of the surrounding world and acquired skills spread among kin and tribal groups and thus helped to develop functional ties within such communities as cities, states and nations. This stage was already reached by the major cultures of antiquity, some of which have persisted to our times.

After Christianity became widely estabilished greater prominence was achieved by man's tendency to improve his limited abilities through voluntary associations under joint leadership often formed by men of some particular skill. The communities of monks of the order of St. Benedict, who assembled to pray and work together, laid the foundations of European culture. Processes that began a thousand years later led to the rise of a world market and to industrialization, giving birth to thousands of cultural, political and other associations. These social groups have enough power to reach across frontiers and to change the spatial social structure of mankind, while their persistence and viability is usually much greater than that of ancestral — e.g. dynastic — traditions.

The three stages outlined above allow us to draw a schematic pattern for the development of culture and also to use this criterion for classifying the cultures existing today according to the domination of feminine or masculine traits.

## Tentative Schematic Classification

| Stages of development (Types of culture) | Variety dominated by feminine traits |
| --- | --- |
| *First stage* Cultures concerned with perpetuation of values (time) | *Totems and clans.* Homogeneous communities distinguished by objects taken from nature — totems — with which they remain in a consciously established relation. The consciousness, transferred from generation to generation, perpetuates the clan's existence. Time is perceived as the succession of generations, i.e. the rhythm of recurring changes, which corresponds to the concept *chronos.* |
| *Second stage* Cultures introducing exchange of goods and widening their social space | *Culturally complex functional structures.* Communities formed functionally according to totems, kin and tribal groups, occupations, estate, caste, etc. Development of city centres, public assemblies, bartering markets, contractual relations, common laws. Further growth of nation, etc. Stability in such structures depends on confidence in the functioning of their elements — on what may be called "objective truthfulness". |
| *Third stage* Cultures enhancing the ability to implement selected values and development | *Voluntary associations.* Associations with voluntary membership, differently organized and for different aims connected with the particular domains of social life. Their activities depend on the initiative, dynamism and abilities of the leaders, also on involvement and discipline of the members. Let us call them the "basis" of social life. |

| Stages of development (Types of culture) | Variety dominated by masculine traits |
|---|---|
| *First stage* Cultures concerned with perpetuation of values (time) | *Heroes, kin-groups.* Leaders initiating new ways in the life of a community and enshrined in communal memory. The spiritual and material heritage allows one to determine the turning point in the rhythm of changes. Unique events originate the history of a kin-group or tribe. The time suitable for such events corresponds to the connotations of the term *kairos.* |
| *Second stage* Cultures introducing exchange of goods and widening their social space | *Rulers, states, legislation.* Individuals and groups that dominate others; they raise armies, apply coercion, develop vertical power structures dominating increasingly differentiated communities, enact laws and issue decrees. The authority of rulers depends on the stability of the thus developed social space; it rests on the harmony of words and deeds — on what may be termed "subjective truthfulness". |
| *Third stage* Cultures enhancing the ability to implement selected values and development | *Institutions, ideologies, programs, theories.* Endeavour to explain certain domains or all social relations with one comprehensive system. Attempts to confer one integrating genetic code upon culture, to make culture subservient to one ideology. |

55

## 3. *Evil and its Polarization in Culture*

An one-sided, either feminine or masculine outlook on the world is a threat to any so-afflicted culture. The societies that develop in the absence of either of the mutually complementary varieties of reception are badly stunted morally. This applies to all the three stages of culture development distinguished here, but particularly to the last one because of its tendency to accumulate what is sometimes referred to as "social sins" or "structural sins" from earlier periods.

3.1. The starting point for the process of disruption in culture is usually an over-emphasis on the *feminine side*. It manifests itself by:

— a growing preoccupation with the search for material goods in the surrounding world, leading to consumer attitudes, luxury, hedonism;
— feeling of superiority of kin-groups, cities (polis), social classes, languages, cultures, races, nations, combined with contempt of others;
— exploitation of weaker economic and political structures, leading to their decay, aimed at multiplication of wealth and technical superiority.

"Consumer atheism" constitutes the secondary result of such one-sideness. Members of the above-described social groups are more and more indifferent to God; they consider themselves sufficiently able to create a "humanistic" world that is comfortable for them and free of an excessive number of people. Religious notions and symbols are becoming relics of history.

3.2. Transformations of culture leading towards one-sideness of a *masculine type* are usually stimulated by the rich and comfortable life-style of others. For thousands of years masculine conquerors subordinated to them members of rich societies of urban, mercantile culture. Modern masculine-type cultures can be characterized in the following way:

— economic, political and military oligarchies strive to subordinate to them all population as working force, or political subjects, or source of draftees and the like;

— any convenient ideology, theory or threat is employed in order to subordinate people and to rule them;

— fruits of common work are used as the means for consolidation of power and expansion of imperium, for launching wars and instigating revolutions, for support of coups and terrorism, etc.

As the consequence of such one-sideness in cultural transformations, independent social centres (that is, political, professional and religious associations) are restricted or even liquidated and institutional atheism is being developed.

3.3. The polarization of the masculine and the feminine macrostructures has now reached a stage which brings to the mind images from the Apocalypse. Those images, however, are in a way independent of time and place: they can be referred to different periods in history or different cultures and even to very limited, small social groups. Even within familes there is often a one-sided domination either of the materialistic, feminine modes of behaviour aimed at luxury and hedonism or, on the contrary, of the distorted patriarchal ways of the husband who ruthlessly forces his life-style of material pursuits, his immoral behaviour or his political beliefs on his wife and the rest of the family demanding that they follow in his wake. To brand individuals, small groups or even whole countries as "harlots" or "beasts" may, however, cause the wheat of the Gospel to be rooted up together with the tares. Between the two extremes of "ideal types", deliberately so sharply contrasted here, extends a whole range of intermediate categories. An understanding from this point of view of the differences distinguishing nations where the Church inculturates the Gospel may be helpful in the practical appraisal of actual situations.

## 4. *The Gospel and the Integration of Culture*

4.1. The disfunction implanted by sin into the masculine and feminine elements of human personality refers to interpersonal relations as well as to man's inner structure. Sex is determined through the flesh but does not determine the soul, which by its powers continually transcends this division. Jesus shows us in His personality and in His teaching that new fulness of human nature which has precedence over the masculine or the feminine spiritual traits. With such completeness there is no "rib" missing from the spiritual "skeleton" of human nature: it then completely controls the body regardless of sex. In the Sermon on the Mount, particularly in the beatitudes (Mt. 5:1-10), Jesus Christ defined concisely the complete human nature. The moral code of everyone who wants to believe and imitate Jesus has to comprise all the precepts contained in all eight beatitudes. On the other hand, the contribution of even the greatest of saints to the culture often amounted to no more than a single one of the beatitudes. If so, we can discuss each of them separately and not necessarily all eight together. Compliance with each of these invocations contributes to a particular domain of culture. When considered together the invocations refer to the whole of the question discussed in this paper. To support this view the eight beatitudes have been here arranged in pairs, the first four opposite the other four:

| | |
|---|---|
| the poor in spirit | – the merciful |
| those who mourn | – the pure of heart |
| the patient | – the peace-makers |
| those who hunger and thirst for holiness | – those who suffer persecution in the cause of right. |

The arrangement of the beatitudes four by four seems justified since St Luke listed only the first four of them (Luke 6:20 f.), those that refer to the manner of perception and utilization of existing values, world order and culture. These first four beatitudes I consider receptive, i.e. corresponding to the feminine approach to culture. St Matthew listed also the other four, those that define the active way of participating in the formation of culture. I consider these directive, i.e. representing the masculine approach to culture. The integration of culture requires both sides of the symmetry to be accounted for, just as in individual life all eight beatitudes integrate the personality of a saint.

Each of the pairs of beatitudes applies to a different type of culture described earlier (Part 3 above).

4.2. Poverty in spirit and mercifulness are the guide-lines of a Christian's being. The inclination to use only those wordly goods that are necessary to satisfy real needs (without aspiring for material things that others have and that are required solely to embellish one's position) rejects the influence of consumerism and welcomes the light of the spiritual and not only the material achievements of culture. The attitude of mercifulness should be the distinctive trait of a Christian's external activities. It means sensitivity to and perceptivity of other people's real needs and willingess to satisfy these needs regardless of who and what those people are. In a broader sense this consists not only in aid offered to individuals, but also in all actions aimed at satisfying any morally justified needs of others. Examples may be the great discoveries recorded in history that serve mankind; any ordinary everyday work done to provide things useful to others; the work of a nurse who cares equally about all her patients even if, for example, some of them are criminals. It may be said of an employee who renders services to those in need or of a producer who has no knowledge and no control of the destination of what he manufactures, that when he follows the precepts of good work he imitates our "Father in heaven, who makes ... his rain fall on the just and equally on the unjust" (Mt. 5:45).

4.3. Mourning and a pure heart are precepts telling how to participate in social structures. Truth is the bond uniting people in the social space delimitated by families, nations and governments. People who mourn are: wifes dominated by their husbands; those who have been conquered and subjugated by others; the mourning are also those who have been assigned the meanest tasks and functions in society; those who suffer injustice, who are defamed, who are driven out to an inferior social position; people with moral authority, recognized intellectuals and experts barred from performing their proper functions; the sick, the aged, the disabled and the destitute who receive no aid. Also among the mourning ought to be counted the nations and the people who are self-complacent about their abilities, their contribution to world culture or to the welfare of their society, who feel fate has always been unfair to them. The evangelical attitude to mourning thus means an inner consent to accept unfavourable positions or even "the last place" in public life, restraint in judging one's own contribution to common welfare, watchfulness as to one's mistakes and alertness to criticism.

Persons and groups who are pure of heart are concerned with the good and the welfare of others; they serve the community specially when they act as leaders. They are then attentive to the needs of the community and not to their own comfort, profit, prestige and the expanding of their achievements or their power. They are not hypocrites in the sense of Scribes and Pharisees (Mt. 23:13 f). The pure heart represents the stand that precludes the subjugation of others, also subjugation masked by a formal consent extracted under duress or without awareness of consequences. Purity or cleanness of heart is often referred only to relations between sexes and to marriage, but in fact it applies to all kinds of interpersonal relations and implies concord of thought, words and deeds.

Social space should be constituted by that range of interpersonal relations which, on the one hand, is characterized by the truthfulness of the humble, often unappreciated persons "who mourne" and, on the other hand, by the truthfulness of persons, who as leaders or in position of authority seek to serve those in their care and to improve subjective civic relations. It is on such attitudes that the cohesion of the micro- and macrostructures in social space is based.

4.4. Patience and peace-making are the preconditions, on which the viability of culture and the dynamism of its growth depend. Those farmers, workers, craftsmen, professionals, etc., who work for other people, I consider the Gospel patient who has been promised "the possession of the land". In countless estabilishments groups of employees create fruits of culture. These fruits, as time and transformations go on, are produced by a growing number of partial producers. This leads to the process in which all the above-mentioned employees participate less and less in decisions regarding the destination of their product.

Disposers of the product of intellectual as well as material nature, on the contrary, can influence its destination. They decide whether the product is used to satisfy justified needs of other people or to deepen social inequalities and intensify all kinds of aggression and enslavement.

I called peace-makers those disposers (or those who influence disposition) of the social product, who try to distribute it in a way that narrows the distances among peoples and nations and brings them together rather than divides them. Living culture, culture as a whole and in all its particular domains, blossoms through the cooperation of, on the one hand, the poor in spirit, the humble (the mourning) experts and the patient rank-and-fils workers united in a common effort with, on the other hand, the merciful, the pure of heart organizers and leaders who direct the social product to peaceful goals and "shall be counted the children of God" (Mt. 5:9).

4.5. The last pair of beatitudes requires a more extensive examination. In the analysis here presented of the cleavage of culture and the significance of the beatitudes there is no mention of the Decalogue. The Ten Commandments, which codify the moral law common to all people, sufficed to deal with the social problems at the time when the sons of Abraham were just entering upon the epoch of building their own social space. Jesus at the very beginning of His preaching said, "The appointed time has come, and the kingdom of God is near at hand; repent and believe the gospel" (Mk.1:15). Thus Jesus told us that history had come to a turning point. In the division of historical epochs made earlier, in this paper this special point in the development of culture corresponds to the end of the epoch when the problems of constructing social space were being mastered. At the time of Jesus the Jews were already formed into a well developed, multifunctional and complex society with its own culture — i.e. a nation. This is evidenced by the fact that even after the dispersal they have maintained their identity through two millenia to our times. The Roman empire, which then ruled over Palestine, had developed to perfection its legal system and its organization, so much so that it has been viewed ever since as a classical model. It is then that in the Mediterranean Basin the third stage of cultural development was just beginning; men and women were involved in consciously and unrestrictedly building the structures of social life that would be continually enriched. In parallel the influence of the spreading of moral evil on the polarization of culture has been strengthened to the extent that today we live with the real danger of mankind's self-destruction.

Evil, made possible by the Fall, has caused the disintegration of the masculine and the feminine elements in the human ethos. This in turn has weakened man's culture-building abilities in his striving to master the passing of time, to reach over the space separating people, to overcome inertia, and to avoid conflicts disrupting dialogue and peace. The weakening of culture-building abilities ultimately results in atheization and secularization in societies, which then cease to yearn for the presence of God and for divine justice, even turning to persecution of those who preach Him.

Generally speaking, the Church's position is the most difficult in countries governed by atheists whose declared policy is to oppose religion. In most of those countries the continuity of the social order has been disrupted by revolution; social structures there are characterized by a deep division between the rulers and the governed; all associations for common action, including religious communities, are submitted to centrally coordinated controls. The Christians of those countries, particularly the ones who do not hide their beliefs, can practise only the first four of the beatitudes: to be poor not only of necessity but also in spirit; to mourn since they have access only to the humblest of social functions; to be patient since even when they show creative initiative in their usually lowly posts they are not listened to; to hunger for holiness since in most cases they suffer from insufficient contacts with religion and the Church.

In most of the rich and democratic countries, on the other hand, there is no segregation between believers and atheists; moral evil resulting from a one-sided domination by the feminine factor in culture affects the attitudes of the whole population and reaches people more from the inside than in societies submitted to atheist control; the Christian is free to practise charity, to act as the subject from motives of a pure heart, to engage in efforts bringing people together in order to preserve peace, and to work for justice in the poor exploited countries. It seems, however, that he has much trouble with opposing the social pressures of the praxis of rich societies: the luxury of ostentatious consumerism as opposed to poverty in spirit; aggressive competition as opposed to evangelical mourning; preference for very profitable armament production as opposed to evangelical patience. Religion then may become merely an element of social rhetoric and only exceptionally be reflected in the hunger and thirst for justice, i.e. in a desire to know and follow the Gospel.

The inculturation of the Gospel necessitates at first that it is rooted in the feminine attitudes. Faith accepted by individuals and communities springs from listening to the Word of God. The choice and the interiorization of the values found in the surrounding world mark the feminine attribute; in theology this is expressed by the tenet that the people of God are "the bride of Christ". Once rooted in a culture the local Church generates her own vocations to the ministry and embarks upon missionary work; it is then that the masculine attributes appear. This is why the foundations, without which inculturation of the Gospel withers away, consist of the practical application of the invocations from the first four beatitudes; for by limiting himself to mere necessities man finds it easier to turn his attention to his neighbour and to God.

The point of view adopted in this paper has its origin in the historical experience and the present situation of my country. For centuries Poland has been the meeting point of East and West, and to some extent also of North and South. The people living here, whose ethical and cultural identity extends back over millenia, have been exposed to different, criss-crossing cultural influences; the present Christian praxis is not unimpeded but has to cope with problems characteristic for both the East and the West, though only some of those impediments do actually occur. It is thus possible for religion to be independent and to be widely viewed as a valid cultural alternative. This situation seems to favour reflection and the formation of general and comparative judegments.

ANDRZEJ SWIĘCICKI

Finito di stampare il 13 marzo 1992
Tipografia Poliglotta della Pontificia Università Gregoriana
Piazza della Pilotta, 4 – 00187 Roma